THE UNFILMED ORIGINAL SCREENPLAY BY LORRAINE HANSBERRY OF HER AWARD-WINNING PLAY
A RAISIN IN THE SUN

"One of the handful of great American plays—it belongs in the inner circle, along with *Death of a Salesman, Long Day's Journey Into Night,* and *The Glass Menagerie.*"
—*Washington Post*

"A classic, a play rooted in its own time that speaks through the years to our own . . . it reaches into the heart of everyone who sees it."
—*Chicago Tribune*

"Never before in the entire history of the American theater has so much of the truth of Black people's lives been seen on the stage."
—James Baldwin

"A major event in the American theater . . . a beautiful, extraordinarily moving drama."
—*Cue* magazine

LORRAINE HANSBERRY electrified the theatrical world with her first play, *A Raisin in the Sun*, which won the New York Critics Circle Award for the 1958–59 season. Before her tragic death from cancer at the age of 34, she had already produced a remarkable body of work, including *The Sign in Sidney Brustein's Window* and *Les Blancs.* Her former husband and literary executor, the late Robert Nemiroff, posthumously produced and published her *To Be Young, Gifted and Black* and the musical *Raisin. A Raisin in the Sun* has been translated into 30 languages and is considered a true classic of the American theater.

A RAISIN IN THE SUN

THE UNFILMED ORIGINAL SCREENPLAY

LORRAINE HANSBERRY

Edited by Robert Nemiroff

Foreword by Jewell Handy Gresham-Nemiroff
Introduction by Margaret B. Wilkerson

With a Commentary by Spike Lee

A PLUME BOOK

PLUME
Published by the Penguin Group
Penguin Books USA Inc., 375 Hudson Street,
New York, New York 10014, U.S.A.
Penguin Books Ltd, 27 Wrights Lane,
London W8 5TZ, England
Penguin Books Australia Ltd, Ringwood,
Victoria, Australia
Penguin Books Canada Ltd, 10 Alcorn Avenue,
Toronto, Ontario, Canada M4V 3B2
Penguin Books (N.Z.) Ltd, 182–190 Wairau Road,
Auckland 10, New Zealand

Penguin Books Ltd, Registered Offices:
Harmondsworth, Middlesex, England

First published by Plume, an imprint of New American Library,
a division of Penguin Books USA Inc.
Simultaneously published in a Dutton hardcover edition.

First Printing, October, 1992
10 9 8 7 6 5 4 3 2 1

 REGISTERED TRADEMARK—MARCA REGISTRADA

LIBRARY OF CONGRESS CATALOGING-IN-PUBLICATION DATA:
Hansberry, Lorraine, 1930–1965.
A raisin in the sun : the unfilmed original screenplay / Lorraine
Hansberry ; edited by Robert Nemiroff ; foreword by Jewell Gresham
Nemiroff ; introduction by Margaret B. Wilkerson, with an afterword
by Spike Lee.
    p.   cm.
ISBN 0-452-26776-5
I. Nemiroff, Robert. II. Title.
PN1997.R2259 1992
812'.54—dc20   92-53556
                                                         CIP

Printed in the United States of America
Set in Times Roman

PUBLISHER'S NOTE
This is a work of fiction. Names, characters, places, and incidents either are the product
of the author's imagination or are used fictitiously, and any resemblance to actual persons,
living or dead, events, or locales is entirely coincidental.

In memoriam

ROBERT NEMIROFF
1929–1991

CONTENTS

FOREWORD
by Jewell Handy Gresham-Nemiroff

If anything should happen—before 'tis done—may
I trust that all commas and periods will be placed
and someone will complete my thoughts—
          —Lorraine Hansberry, undated journal entry

When 34-year-old Lorraine Hansberry died at 8:30 A.M. on
Tuesday, January 12, 1965, she was still—five years following the 1959 landmark appearance of her first play on
Broadway—the youngest American, the fifth woman, and
the first and only African American to win the coveted
Best American Play award from the prestigious New York
Drama Critics Circle. The small band of influential men
who anointed her did so in a season that featured new
works by Tennessee Williams and Archibald MacLeish and
a revival of a play by Eugene O'Neill.

For the moment we will move past the fact that only a
handful of women* preceded Hansberry in being so hon-
ored; nonetheless, the question remains that might appro-
priately have been asked at the time Hansberry's work
appeared: Why did it take so long for an authentic aspect

*Women who preceded Hansberry: 1941, Lillian Hellman, *Watch on the Rhine;*
1950, Carson McCullers, *The Member of the Wedding;* 1956, Frances Goodrich
(with Albert Hackett), *The Diary of Anne Frank;* 1958, Ketti Frings, *Look
Homeward, Angel.* The number of African American playwrights winning acclaim in the American theater since Hansberry is much more noteworthy
today.

of the black American experience to be presented as serious drama on the American stage?

The question seems the more relevant in light of the cultural truth pointed out by W. E. B. Du Bois in *The Souls of Black Folk* more than a half century earlier, namely, that African Americans are so richly possessed by the spirit of song, which is to say of poetry, the fount of all art. It is an endowment, Du Bois explains, that arises not from genetics but from a profound acquaintance with sorrow and a resulting affinity for its companion on the reverse side of the coin, joy.

Why did it take so long? Certainly in the years between Du Bois and Hansberry, as the American theater came of age, there were many gifted black writers capable of creating dramas rich in meaning for themselves and others out of the stuff of their everyday lives and dreams.

The answer to the question has to do with the realities of the nation's history, past and present: with the customs and traditions, for instance, that led up to *Birth of a Nation* and *Gone with the Wind* standing today as supreme mythological and filmic icons in American culture. This exemplifies a vast and tragic chasm between black and white experience.

The answer, then, also has to do with the reason that *A Raisin in the Sun* was Hansberry's first play. It was her intention to get beyond (paraphrasing her) the cultural portrayal of black Americans that was a norm in American life: as exotic, bestial, silly, or sullen—biologically criminal on the one hand or comically simpleminded on the other—in short, the plethora of dehumanizing images callously or sometimes merely carelessly superimposed day after day on the psyches and lives of black (and white) people.

In his 1975 interpretive history of blacks in American films, film historian Donald Bogle indicated through his title, *Toms, Coons, Mulattoes, Mammies & Bucks*, some of the vicious culturally imposed labels still persisting today.

Hansberry knew these well and shuddered at how, in themselves, they embodied the ugly stereotypes of the society. All artists who genuinely ply their trade shudder at human and cosmic horrors; it has been part of the tradition of the theater ever since the Greek tragedians.

This being so, there comes a time in history when one triumphs simply by eloquently portraying the obvious—and in the case of Hansberry, by persisting in doing so on her own terms in the face of entrenched traditions to the contrary.

For her first play, this artist identified her immediate motivation as the need to portray her people as she knew them to be: human beings with conflicts, dreams, aspirations, foibles and strengths; the corrupted and the pure in heart, collectively possessing the will to create and overcome in the face of odds that severely try and frequently destroy body and soul.

Having originally brought this truth into dramatic form for the stage through the realistic and poetic portrayal of the dreams of a struggling working class Chicago black family, when the chance came to "open up" her play through the medium of film, she sought to go further. Keenly conscious of the capability of cinematic form to capture *immensity,* she intended to write a screenplay that would project not merely the realities but the *epic* dimensions of the lives and world of the characters she had created. To visualize this, she had to possess a powerful cosmic sense of the magnitude of human struggle in the modern world waged by ordinary men and women. Such battles against themselves and others, against wretchedness, and against fate she believed to be of comparable worth as dramatic material to the woes of ancient kings and queens in whom grave flaws of character inevitably led to disaster.

But there was also another and even more profound difference in the classical tradition as drawn upon by this African American artist removed in time, space, and experience from the Greeks and Shakespeare. For her, the moment in human history *had* to come when the fateful principle of "recognition" of the catastrophic ends inherent in human arrogance and folly could occur—*must* occur *before* their course becomes irrevocable.

In an article in the *Village Voice* ("Reflections of an Author," August 12, 1959), she wrote triumphantly of Walter Lee Younger, her male protagonist in *A Raisin in the Sun*. For in the climactic moments of the play, this chauffeur and son of a laborer recovers and saves himself—in the name of his family and an entire people—from submitting, for money, to collaboration in an American dream that held them worthless:

> . . . If there are not waving flags and marching songs at the barricades as Walter marches out with his little battalion, it is not because the battle lacks nobility. On the contrary, he has picked up in his way, still imperfect and wobbly in his small view of human destiny, what I believe Arthur Miller once called "the golden thread of history." He becomes, in spite of those who are too intrigued with despair and hatred of man to see it, King Oedipus refusing to tear out his eyes but attacking the oracle instead. He is that last Jewish patriot manning his rifle in the burning ghetto at Warsaw; he is that young girl who swam into sharks to save a friend a few weeks ago; he is Anne Frank, still believing in people; he is the nine small heroes of Little Rock; he is Michelangelo creating David and Beethoven bursting forth with the Ninth Symphony. He is all those things because he has finally reached in his tiny moment and caught that sweet essence which is human dignity, and it shines like the old star-touched dream.

So it is not only a realistic picture of the lives and dreams of the Younger family that Hansberry wished to enhance in her screenplay but quite specifically the *magnitude* of her characters, their struggles, and crises. She wanted to show the capacity of human beings for transcendence and triumph through victories that, no matter how seemingly minuscule, are of tremendous significance in the order (and disorder) of the universe.

For reasons discussed by Margaret Wilkerson in her Introduction and Spike Lee in his Commentary, the film as envisioned by Hansberry in her script never emerged on screen. When she died in 1965, those members of the public who mourned her passing knew her as the gifted author of one successful play—*A Raisin in the Sun*—and another, *The Sign in Sidney Brustein's Window*, that closed to mixed reviews on Broadway even as the playwright's own life ended. People sighed that it was too bad her brief lifespan had not given her time to fulfill such obvious promise.

Now in 1992, as the unfilmed screenplay is being published for the first time, behind its appearance more than three decades after the original film version there lies a story as full of drama, of irony, of struggles and triumphs—and pain—quite in keeping with the vision of the artist and her assuredness about the strength and persistence of the human spirit.

When Robert Nemiroff died on July 18, 1991, one of the last projects he was working on was publication of this unfilmed script of *A Raisin in the Sun*, brought by him into its final stages even as his illness progressed. At 61, he had survived by twenty-six years the gifted playwright to whom he was joined in 1952—he at 23, she a year younger—in a marriage that ended in 1964. But the dissolution of the marital bonds did not affect in any way the creative partnership that marked the marriage and extended beyond it to the date of Nemiroff's death.

It was my privilege to share the last twenty-five years of the life of the man more responsible than any other single individual for getting Hansberry's work before a broad array of audiences, and—patiently, persistently, tenaciously—keeping it there in all its rich variety until public and critical awareness of the stature of this writer was achieved.

This foreword is written in tribute to Bob Nemiroff, for it is no small feat to add to our knowledge of human culture and our appreciation of the invaluable role of the artist.

Death can be conquered only by snatching some form of triumph from it, to keep the loss from being total. To lose an artist with the perceptive vision and powers of fancy, logic, and articulation of Lorraine Hansberry when African Americans and the nation so desperately needed her to "bear witness," as James Baldwin so eloquently put it, could be compensated for only by making that voice heard past her death.

Ironically, Bob died at the same New York hospital, of the same cruel disease, after just about the same period of illness, as Hansberry had before him.

Though he had made it much further along the way, he had not reached the biblical allotment of three score years and ten. He was, at 61, a vigorous man of easy temperament and zany good humor, and his going, too, was cruelly premature.

Quite aware of the cosmic absurdities that mark the human condition, in a very real way he snatched his own triumph from life before he died, in the life's work of articulating and affirming one artist's achievement to her culture and times and beyond. His task, as he saw it, was to secure the place of the Hansberry legacy in American drama and letters by revealing its breadth and depth and the multiple dimensions of the artist's gifts.

He never envisioned that it would become a life's work; he thought that what he contemplated could be completed within a decade.

He was wrong. However multifaceted Hansberry's talents, she was first and foremost a dramatist. Drama as genre occurs in two forms: as scripts to be transformed into living characters and events on stage or screen and as literary works, printed and read. What Bob faced was the dual task, first of getting and keeping the playwright's works constantly performed (given the economics of the stage, not easy!) and second, getting and keeping all her literary contributions not merely in print but widely disseminated through multiple channels. With these essentials effected, he knew very well that the power and beauty of the artist's writing would take over from there.

In a biographical note, he defined his responsibilities as being

> . . . to focus as much as possible, for the time being and within the limits of economic necessity, on the legacy she had left . . . several file cabinets full of manuscripts and writings in many genres and varying stages of completion. As her literary executor entrusted by the writer with sole responsibility for the future of a body of work which I considered to be an important and quite possibly major literary and historical resource, I felt it incumbent upon me to do what I could to see that, insofar as possible, those works that merited it were edited and adapted for production in the media for which they were intended, and that the papers were organized, edited, annotated, and published for the use of the current generation as well as future scholars.

Bob's background as award-winning songwriter, music publisher and editor—and his genius for organizing ideas to share with others served his mission well. So did (perhaps above all else) his ability to involve other people in projects he initiated because the undertakings mattered profoundly.

The result is that there may be no other American artist for whom so many people have played a direct role after her death in "placing the commas and periods" and helping to "complete" the thoughts.* So, while it is correct enough to say that Hansberry's literary executor is the individual most responsible for beginning the process, literally multitudes of people form the ranks of the co-participants who in the end matter most—among them the now innumerable audiences who have seen her plays and African American audiences in particular who bear witness for her over and over again.

Any person who has a passionate commitment to art and artists—and the world they affirm—is inherently a critic, cultural analyst, and historian. Where Hansberry was concerned, Bob was all that. His introductions to her plays for the reading public and the meticulous notes he provided for the acting versions are revealing and enhancing. Likewise, his critical analyses and explorations with scholars, critics, and interested journalists add up to a fascinating body of work.

The result in the case of *A Raisin in the Sun* is an invaluable record of what I suspect may be the only consistently maintained history of the progression of a single American play, repeatedly performed across the country and in thirty languages abroad.

For the 25th anniversary of *A Raisin in the Sun*, Bob restored cuts made for various reasons when the play opened on Broadway. Following the triumph of the fully restored version—and the PBS presentation on television viewed by one of the largest audiences in the history of the network—it is no accident that he saw the current moment as the strategic time to follow with an example of Hans-

---

*Affirmation of the artist in this special sense began even as her bout with cancer became critical shortly after *The Sign in Sidney Brustein's Window* opened on Broadway. The galaxy of luminaries of the stage and related professions joining the audiences who spontaneously rallied to help save the play is too numerous to list here; their names are included in Bob's compelling account of "The 101 'Final' Performances of Sidney Brustein's Window," which along with British novelist John Braine's essay, "A 'Great' Play—Sidney Brustein—No Other Word Is Possible," introduces the published version of the play (New York: Plume, 1987).

berry's vision for African Americans in film as it existed three decades before.

The following is taken from his Notes on the screenplay:

The Hansberry screenplay is in no sense a repeat or slightly expanded version of the stageplay, and it is vastly different from the 1961 movie, which was essentially the stageplay with minor "openings out." At least forty percent of the text (not counting smaller variations within speeches—there are hundreds of these) is brand new, containing what all who've read it recently recognize as some of her finest (and most startlingly contemporary) writing: new scenes heighten the drama, expand our understanding of what the play is all about and the realities of the ghetto the Youngers are struggling to transcend and, most strikingly, anticipate the revolution in black and national consciousness the next decades would bring.

I'm referring here to the dialogue . . . but also, indeed above all, to the purely cinematic—the imagery—because Lorraine, as it happens, was and had always been as intrigued and fascinated by the art and form of film as with the stage. While retaining the primary scenes, themes, and dialogue of the play, therefore, she sought to capture through the camera what the stageplay could only *talk* about: the full reality of the ghetto experience not isolated from but within the larger society that shapes, confines, and goads the Youngers.

It is timely, therefore, that the unfilmed screen version of Hansberry's stage play—now canonized as an American classic—should reach the public now. It does so as a handful of young African American male filmmakers are having a significant impact within the legendary citadel of celluloid hyperfantasizing and mythmaking known as Hollywood. Interestingly enough, these in turn are influencing young English directors of Jamaican origin seeking to play a similar kind of role in their setting and beyond.

To appreciate the regularity of developments through which Hansberry's works, new and revived, emerged by Bob's efforts, one would have to examine the meticulous records he maintained as Hansberry's literary executor in line with his respect for scholarship and posterity.

The strategically conceived point of departure for his early efforts was his own creation of *To Be Young, Gifted and Black: Lorraine Hansberry in Her Own Words*, first staged as a play in 1969 and expanded into a book the same year. The title was taken from the climax of Hansberry's last speech, delivered for the winners of a creative writing contest sponsored by the United Negro College Fund.

The 1969 Off-Broadway drama was the longest running of the year. With four touring companies on the road, it subsequently ran from 1970 through 1972, with performances at over 270 colleges and other institutions (including the Library of Congress) in forty-one states. Subsequently, it was adapted for film and television and is today regularly performed in community theaters, schools, and colleges.

There is no question but that the widespread dissemination of this imaginatively structured sampling of Hansberry's words, ideas, and style provided the foundation from which it was possible thereafter to keep works by and about her available.

The result is that no published work by this writer is out of print, and productions of her plays are constantly to be seen on various stages—professional and amateur— at home and, in the case of *A Raisin in the Sun*, abroad.

Hansberry's greatest gift to Bob was that, through her creativity, she gave him access to the magic of theater that had been since his graduate work in literary criticism and theater at New York University his deepest love. For him, the theater was forever exciting and rewarding whatever the frustrations attendant upon the economics of the professional stage. By the same token (despite the vicissitudes of being involved with any arts community) he regarded the theatrical community as among the most gifted, humane, and nurturing.

His greatest gift to Hansberry was his faith in the dramatic and literary outpourings of this woman who had declared to him with certainty: "I am a writer. I am going to write!" and his sustained commitment, with the writer prematurely gone, to make certain that what she wrote would live.

But it is worth noting that, in the ultimate sense, Bob's ultimate commitment was also to the theater and what this institution can represent for society in affirmation of the human condition. I have seen him—as various of Hansberry's plays were performed across the country— take full advantage of the invitations to talk to the artistic and business directors of regional theaters, to the radio and television audiences of entertainment and talk shows, to English and drama teachers and students, and to various community groups including, in the African American community, ministers and fledgling grassroots artistic organizations.

He did not live to complete the task of seeing through to production or publication all of Hansberry's works worthy of such exposure. When he died, between productions, he was working on rounding out one or more final volumes of the artist's unpublished works.

He did live to witness—following the triumphant twenty-fifth anniversary productions of *A Raisin in the Sun* in New York and at Washington's Kennedy Center—the play hailed by David Richards in the *Washington Post* as "one of the handful of great American dramas . . . in the inner circle along with *Death of a Salesman*, *Long Day's Journey into Night*, and *The Glass Menagerie*. Richards joined several New York critics in using the term "classic" in their reviews.

And when African American poet, playwright, and critic Amiri Baraka wrote an eassy for the *Washington Post* in November 1986 praising *A Raisin in the Sun*'s "profoundly imposing stature, continuing relevance, and pointed social analysis," some of the pain he had quietly known during the Black Power phase of nationalistic black art (when Hansberry was declared by some detractors to be a bourgeois nonrevolutionary artist) was dissipated. For in his judgment, the artist was precisely a revolutionary artist in the avant-garde ranks of her times.

On September 6, 1991, a "Celebration of the Life of Robert Nemiroff" was held at the Brooks Atkinson Theater in New York City. (Coincidentally, the stage was the same on which Bob's own play, *Postmark Zero*, a dramatization of the last German letters to leave Stalingrad during World War II, was produced in 1965 and promptly closed. Whatever the merit of the play, the New York critics did not seem attuned to either the setting or the subject matter.)

The setting at the Brooks Atkinson also suggested other relevant theater history. The house was made available in tribute to Bob by the Nederlander Producing Company. In 1974, from the stage of another Nederlander house, the 46th Street Theater, Bob won the coveted Tony for Best Musical, as producer of the musical *Raisin*.

Receiving a Tony in connection with Hansberry's work was intensely gratifying to Bob. Once more, the characters and vitality of *A Raisin in the Sun* would live on the Broadway stage and thousands of people would be introduced and reintroduced to the playwright.

Ossie Davis and Ruby Dee, one of the most distinguished couples of the American stage, presided at the "Celebration" and immediately evoked an ambience of warmth, beauty, joy, and wonder, joined in and marvelously sustained by the actors, associates, and friends who contributed dramatic offerings, songs, and tributes.

Those of us who loved Bob—and we are many—will try to keep faith with him and his mission of affirmation. As I reviewed *some* of his work (there has not been time for everything) in preparation for writing this piece, I was struck anew by the truth and the poignancy of what the late critic Emery Lewis said about him: "One thing is absolutely certain: the American theater is deeply in debt to this extraordinary man of many talents."

In 1969, when concluding his Acknowledgments—for the published version of *To Be Young, Gifted and Black*—of the dedicated people who contributed to its realization as play and book, Bob stated the following:

> . . . Lastly, a word for my wife, Jewell, who for two years has made this work, and all my life, her own—understanding its importance when others would have doubted and even I was led to hesitate. Without her profound love and belief, the wisdom and joy with which she filled the hours in which this book took shape, and studied its pages, neither it, nor I, could be as you find us now.

Little did I know at the time this tribute was penned that the day would come when it would be turnabout time, and I would feel obliged to pay public tribute to my husband for the man that he was and what he tried to accomplish. This I tried to do in my eulogy in his honor delivered at the "Celebration."

In conclusion, I have no hesitancy in stating that it is fitting—in view of his commitment to the legacy of Lorraine Hansberry as artist and human being—to call upon that shining legacy now and words from *The Sign in Sidney Brustein's Window* that so aptly apply to Bob. Among them are the lines that he had enscribed on the open pages of the "book" that is Hansberry's tombstone. They are, so fittingly, his own epitaph:

Sidney is speaking:

I care. I care about it all. It takes too much energy *not* to care. Yesterday I counted twenty-six gray hairs on the top of my head, all from trying *not* to care. The *why* of why we are here is an intrigue for adolescents; the *how* is what must command the living.

ACKNOWLEDGMENTS

In 1969, when Robert Nemiroff wrote the Acknowledgments for the first edition of *To Be Young, Gifted and Black: Lorraine Hansberry in Her Own Words,* he expressed his gratitude to the people to whom he owed the most for helping to bring the work into being. At this moment in 1992, many of the names on that 1969 roster remain among those who have consistently contributed to Bob's work during all the years since.

Bob's 1969 listing was prefaced with the last line of Hansberry's poignant journal entry voicing the hope that "If anything should happen before 'tis done," someone would place the commas and periods and complete her thoughts. The final line of that brief note was

> This last should be the least difficult—since there are so many who think as I do—

Bob's first acknowledgment at that time was of the late Charlotte Zaltzberg, his secretary, friend, and editorial assistant, for contributing so "creatively and critically" to the book and the play.

The words that followed are still so appropriate today that he is the one who can best speak for himself:

> . . . It is a simple, eloquent fact—and a particular tribute that would, I think, have moved Lorraine perhaps beyond any other—that literally hundreds have helped in these years to preserve and pass on the words she left. They

include many who, like Charlotte, never met Lorraine Hansberry, and others who were amongst her closest friends and comrades; some who indeed "think" as she did—and even some who do not. Each has helped in ways large and small, and collectively they are far too many to enumerate here. . . .

At the same time there are those whose contributions have been so sizable, either directly in terms of the work itself, or indirectly in their assistance or encouragement to me, that of necessity their names cannot be omitted from these pages. At the risk, therefore, of (I fear) inevitably overlooking someone to whom I am especially grateful, . . . I should like to thank the following now:

- My parents, Mae and Motya, . . . my brother Leo, who was the first to teach me most of what I know about writing, . . . and Mili, my sister, who began this work at my side, gave of her great gifts unremittingly, and sustained it through the most difficult times;
- Seymour Baldash, Alan Bomser, . . . Joe Burstin, Jim MacDevitt, and Judd Woldin, whose dedication and friendship have gone so far beyond the purely professional;
- Howard Hausman, the first agent I ever met who proved not a "necessary evil," but a true friend of art;
- James Baldwin, who believed and brought his special eloquence to these pages;
- . . . Alvin Epstein, . . . Lillian and Frank Jaros, . . . Edith and Samuel Kamen, John and Grace Killens, . . . Judy and Irving Lerner . . . David and Judy Nemiroff . . . Rabbi Michael Robinson, Norma Rodgers, . . . Harold Scott, Joseph Stein, . . . Cora and Peter Weiss, . . .
- . . . the staff and volunteer workers of the embattled but eternally venturesome WBAI . . . [and the] distinguished artists who gave so magnificently, freely and lovingly of their time and talent to the . . . first public presentation of many of the words in this book;
- *And seven for whom no words can suffice:* Ossie Davis and Ruby Dee, Burt and Art D'Lugoff, Estelle Frank, Edith Gordon and Ray Larsen. . . .

In 1992, it is necessary to add to Bob's original list—and to *reemphasize* certain names, beginning with Dr. Burton D'Lugoff, the man who fought with all his might—as friend, colleague, and physician—to save Hansberry in one period and Bob in another from the disease that at last claimed them both. Doctors too have hearts that break.

Max Eisen, Bob's press agent in life and death; Stan Phillips, his artist friend and colleague of long standing; Harriet, Stan's wife; and Joe Bucholtz, whose assistance in the wake of Bob's death was invaluable.

Chiz Schultz, one of the original producers of *To Be Young, Gifted and Black,* who had the painful task of arranging the technical details and staff for the "Celebration." In 1988, Chiz was one of the producers (along with Bob) whose TV production for "American Playhouse" of the 25th anniversary version of *A Raisin in the Sun* was seen by one of the largest audiences in the history of the series.

Director Hal Dewindt, who assisted Chiz.

Art and Avi D'Lugoff who made the Village Gate the setting for the reception at which family and friends gathered to greet each other.

A special word about two special people: Ossie Davis and Ruby Dee. It has been Ossie's lot to eulogize some of the outstanding departed members of the theatrical community and some of the most dynamic figures on the real-life stage of history. It was Ossie who delivered the powerful, lyrical eulogy at the funeral of Malcolm X; Ossie, whose tribute to the late Diana Sands in the *New York Times* following her death placed a comma and period for this gifted actress, who created of the role of Beneatha in the original Broadway production of *A Raisin in the Sun* and who, like Hansberry, departed the earth too soon.

A like measure of gratitude must be expressed to Ruby Dee, Ossie's life partner and co-creator in the worlds of the stage and screen and writing. It was Ruby Dee who created the role of Ruth in the original Broadway production of *A Raisin in the Sun.* I am most grateful to this lyrically gifted actress and poet for presiding with Ossie at the "Celebration."

Space does not permit adequate expression of my thanks to the other actors who contributed so immeasurably to the "Celebration." Among them: Delroy Lindo and Kim Yancy, who played, for the 25th anniversary of *A Raisin in the Sun,* the roles originally played by Sidney Poitier and Diana Sands, respectively. And John Fiedler, who played the role of Lindner in the original and found it a labor of love to return the second time around.

Thanks also to Ernestine Jackson, who played the role of Ruth in the Broadway production of the musical *Raisin*, and actor Herb Downer, also from the musical.

Space also cuts short my expression of gratitude to Bob's closest friends and associates. First, singer and composer Ernie Lieberman; Ann Lieberman, his wife; and Clarence Jones.

Samuel (Biff) Liff, his agent, for friendship and dedication going far beyond the usual relationships between agent and client; Judd Woldin, the composer of the musical *Raisin,* who first brought Bob the idea that a musical could be made faithful to the original play and worthy of it. And Amy Seidman.

Howard Hausman, and his wife Marie, for consistent manifestation of sensitivity, intellect, and imagination that enriches the world; Mamie Hansberry Mitchell for supporting Bob's efforts over the years.

Margaret Wilkerson, Hansberry's biographer, whose ready willingness to replace Bob in writing the introduction to this book has so fortunately expedited its completion.

Spike Lee, who responded at once when Bob contacted him, for contributing his thoughts on the screenplay and Hansberry's gifts. Professor Steven Carter, for his 1991 comprehensive scholarly work, *Hansberry's Drama: Creativity Amid Complexity,* which so gratified Bob and validated his faith in others placing commas and periods.

Jean Carey Bond and Esther Jackson, for the 1979 special issue of the journal *Freedomways* entitled *Lorraine Hansberry: Art of Thunder, Vision of Light,* the most comprehensive treatment to that date of works by and about Hansberry.

Zelda Fichhandler, then of Arena Stage, whose dedication in working with Bob to bring the musical into being on that stage represented a giant step toward the ultimate revival of the original play.

Howard Dodson and Roberta Yancey of the Schomburg Center for Research in Black Culture, for their assistance and support after Bob's death, and Arnold Dolin, Senior Vice President and Associate Publisher of NAL/Dutton, for the fidelity with which he has brought into final being the book on which Bob was working when he died.

Estelle Frank and Sol Medoff, patrons without whose early support Bob would not have been able to proceed as expeditiously as he did with his commitment.

And people very close to me who have provided unflagging strength and support: our daughter, Joi Gresham, and her husband Tim Conant; Leo and Mili Nemiroff, my brother and sister-in-law, and their children; Edith Gordon, Ellen Zaltzberg, Joseph and Sophia LaRusso, John and Maryellen DeSilva; my sister, Hattie Manning, brother, Albert Handy, and Cathy, his wife; and my nephew, Paul Nunn.

Finally, additions to the original roster who have played significant roles in the developments leading directly to this publication of the unfilmed screenplay.

It is my belief that, as *To Be Young, Gifted and Black* represented the most compelling work leading to the progressive development of all that has followed, Bob's careful preparation and production of the 25th anniversary version of *A Raisin in the Sun* led to the critical affirmation of Hansberry's play as an American classic.

It is impossible to include the names of all the persons, including the actors and professional staff, who have contributed to the success of 25th (and 30th) anniversary revivals all over the country. Among them, however, the following must be noted.

Todd Haimes of the Roundabout Theatre in New York, who mounted the first revival production; Hal Scott, whose brilliant direction unquestionably contributed to the record-breaking attendance at the Kennedy Center staging that followed; Danny Glover, who sacrified more lucrative screen offers to play the role of Walter Lee in the subsequent PBS television production.

Josie Abady, currently Artistic Director of the Cleveland Players, who, in a discussion of classical works by women that should be revived on screen with the creative casting team of Jaki Brown and Toni Livingston, suggested that they consider *A Raisin in the Sun.*

Brown and Livingston took it from there. Thanks are due Jared Jussim, then of Columbia Pictures, for assisting their efforts and Bob's for the television version eventually realized in the award-winning "American Playhouse" production for PBS.

On behalf of Bob, I am deeply grateful to all the people listed here and to the innumerable others who have played so meaningful a role in placing periods and commas for one of the truly great artists of our times.

—Jewell Handy Gresham-Nemiroff
Croton-on-Hudson, New York
February 1992

INTRODUCTION
by Margaret B. Wilkerson

The 1961 film version of *A Raisin in the Sun* won an award at the Cannes Film Festival and was hailed by critics as a worthy cinematic version of the stage play which won the 1959 New York Drama Critics Circle Award. Lorraine Hansberry was pleased with the result. In an article in the *New York Herald Tribune*, she wrote: "The film which I have finally seen is to me, at least, an extraordinary one. Everywhere in its texture is the devotion and creativity of the gifted cast and of two men: its initial guardian, Philip Rose, and director Dan Petrie."* Hansberry went on to praise Mr. Petrie's "sensitivity . . . and completely successful respect for the *unities of drama* as applied to film" [emphasis added]. Although she concluded that "the result is a thing of beauty," she felt compelled to refer to her original filmscripts (there were two previous versions) in which she abandoned the classical "unities of drama" for a more sweeping vision. "Born to the romance of the Sandburg image of the great city's landscape, I was excited by the opportunity to deal with it visually and sent the formerly housebound characters hither and yon into the city." Most of that location footage ended up on the floor of the cutting room, she states, because her uncut version resulted in over three hours of film.

With the publication of this volume, readers will not only

---

*"What Could Happen Didn't," *New York Herald Tribune*, Lively Arts Section, March 26, 1961, p. 8.

realize the scope of her cinematic vision for the play but will discover that far more than time was cut from the script. A close reading of the *Herald Tribune* article by Hansberry suggests she was being somewhat careful to praise Petrie's ability to film essentially the stage drama, not unlike the achievements of good television filming of stage plays. And although she was apparently pleased with "what he has composed, with genuine pictorial sweep, . . . the rise and fall of the arc of the drama through a stunning filmic eye," the result represented a choice different from her original conception.

It is worth noting that, while critics praised the film for bringing the stage play to millions of viewers and for preserving its fine dramatic qualities—the latter in large part the achievement of the stellar cast who had originated the roles in the Broadway production—most noted that the play remained essentially intact except for a few scenes set outside the confines of the Younger home. That a film like this could achieve any success in 1961 is significant, given the popular movies released during that time: *Gone with the Wind* in its sixth go-around in less than twenty years for an extended run, and Walt Disney's *The Absent-Minded Professor* and *101 Dalmatians* were top money-makers in the same month.

Hansberry's cinematic vision was indeed of Sandburgian sweep as she sought to make her characters quintessential Chicagoans. She wanted to widen the camera's view beyond the cramped Younger apartment to encompass the "City of the Big Shoulders" and its contradictions. The vast financial opportunities and attractive housing of that metropolis are not available to the Youngers, despite their generations of hard work to support the affluent lifestyle of Chicago's privileged. Hansberry, a master of words, willingly sacrificed some of the brilliant dialogue of her stage drama for the eloquence of the visual image. The opening shot was to pan the city landscape of the Southside, the "Negro" part of town, with its overcrowded neighborhoods, children playing in the street for want of a safer playground, and boulevards peopled by the unemployed and the under-employed. In an effective use of the written word as if spo-ken, she imposes Langston Hughes's poem "Harlem," which inspired the title of the work, one line at a time, over the panning shots. Because the poem is an extended question ("What happens to a dream deferred? Does it . . . ?"), this projection of the text as image immediately engages the viewer to "ask" the question that frames the film's thesis. The final phrase, *"Or does it explode?"* hangs over the Southside images as both promise and threat.*

The opening scene of her unfilmed script retains aspects so familiar to this play—the family slowly rising for the day, the simmering quarrel between Walter and Ruth, the warm moments with Travis, their son, the humor of Be-neatha as she counters Walter's criticisms, and finally, the appearance of Lena Younger, family matriarch. After this introduction of the primary characters, and a brief screen moment for Lena, Hansberry's camera focuses on Lena's hands, an image that will be used in the next scenes to "tell" the work history of Lena and women like her: her hands carefully buttoning up the coat of a little girl, the daughter of the white couple for whom she works; her hands immersed in soap suds, washing the child's favorite toy; the sparkling kitchen rendered spotless by her hands. Lena's hands are the hands of the countless laborers who have scrubbed floors, polished silver, combed hair, fixed meals, and in the case of men, dug trenches for railroad ties, built bridges, and chauffeured cars so that Chicago and other cities like it could boast their high standards of living. Through this image, Hansberry connects Lena's work to that of her son, Walter. However, Walter's hands are shown buttoning up his livery coat, while superimposed are images of the lush home of his employer and the district in which he lives, the privileged wife with manicured, jew-

Selected Poems of Langston Hughes (New York: Knopf, 1951), p. 268.

eled hands, and a garage "itself more fit for human habitation." Walter's hands grip a steering wheel or rest idly and impatiently on the dashboard; he is no closer to his family's dreams of opportunity and progress than is his mother. He, too, is part of a domestic staff, with no better-paying job in his future.

Later, as Lena and Walter return home on streetcar or bus from different parts of the city, the camera follows their eyes as each sees the object of their dreams: Lena, a modest, attractive house in a quiet, middle-class neighborhood; Walter, a successful liquor store near his home. Again, the camera pans the neighborhoods, striking a sharp contrast between the places where the Youngers work and where they live. The camera finds Beneatha in the student lounge of the university that she attends, learning Yoruban words from Asagai, her Nigerian friend. Beneatha's concerns about financing her college education offer a counterpoint to the comfort implicit in these surroundings which display the relative leisure of student life (the time to study, to ponder, and to relax).

Before reaching home, Lena stops to buy some apples at a local Southside market, but is angered by a flippant and disrespectful white clerk as well as the poor quality and high price of fruit that, as she says, "was at the Last Supper!" She takes a long bus detour out to the open markets of the far Southside, a Chicago landmark "where the world's finest produce is exhibited for blocks and blocks in the open air," and buys voluptuous apples for a more reasonable price. The economic exploitation of the impoverished Black neighborhoods, seemingly a permanent fixture in urban life, is inescapable in this segment.

Before arriving home, Walter has his own encounter with an unconscious agent of racism when he stops off at Herman's Liquors to ask the owner about the liquor business, and his own interest in investing in a liquor store. In this remarkable scene, Hansberry reveals "the irony of noncommunication between the two men." She writes, in her directorial notes, that "there is nothing 'racist' in Herman's attitude to Walter." He means to be helpful and genuine, but the men are separated by decades of discrimination and deferred dreams. Herman lapses into the typical shopkeeper's complaint about long hours, spendthrift wife, and general hardship. He does not understand that Walter, who has never owned anything much in his life, would welcome such problems so that he could be his own boss and provide for his family as Herman does. Walter, offended by Herman's patronizing attitude, abruptly walks out. The next time Walter is seen on screen, he is drinking with Willy and Bobo, plotting to get part of the insurance money for their investment.

The next scenes move to the Younger interior and include the marvelous moments, though somewhat edited, immortalized by the stage play: the arrival of the $10,000 check, the discovery that Ruth is pregnant and has made a down payment for an abortion, Lena's rejection of Walter's investment proposal, Beneatha's modeling of Asagai's gift and her attempt to dance "African," Walter's angry encounter with George Murchison (Beneatha's date and a personification of bourgeois values), and finally, Lena's revelation that she has used the insurance money to make a down payment on a house for the family.

Walter's disappointment and frustration with his mother's decision are heightened for the viewer by a montage of shots of Walter drinking alone, driving out of the city to the marshlands bordering Lake Calumet, looking at the great steel mills of South Chicago, perusing the stockyards, wandering aimlessly in the downtown Loop amidst the midday crowd, and finally sitting on a curb in the shadow of the Negro Soldier's monument on the Southside. This panorama of possibility, hope, and accomplishment ends with perhaps the most poignant and ironic symbol of African American history and achievement: a monument to men who fought bravely on foreign soil for their country only to be denied at home a share of their nation's promise.

Hansberry's script immediately crystallizes this visual montage in the brilliant street orator scene. Walter wanders onto a street meeting where a middle-aged man in a tired business suit and tie addresses a growing crowd of black people, mostly men. With great sarcasm and to the delight of the crowd, he characterizes their experience—coming from the South to Chicago, "the Promised Land," seeking something better than Mississippi, Georgia, and other Jim Crow states offered, only to be handed a mop and a broom by "the very man who has stolen his homeland, put him in bondage, defamed his nation, robbed him of his heritage!" He compares black Americans to blacks in Africa who are standing up for their rights to self-determination and then asks, "How much has to happen before the black man in the United States is going to understand that God helps those who help themselves? . . . We are the only people in the world who own nothing, who make nothing! . . . Where are your textile or steel mills? Heh? Where are your mighty houses of finance?" In a nice touch, Hansberry places both Asagai, Beneatha's Nigerian friend, and Walter, who have not yet met each other, in the crowd—each with his own reaction. This segment relieves Walter of pleading his own case, as he must during most of the original play and the 1961 film. Walter's frustration is identified with that of many (especially Black men), as the viewers see for themselves the source of Walter's anger and hear from the street orator the harsh sounds of a deferred dream about to explode.

With this prelude, the viewer can readily understand Walter's euphoria when Lena decides to release to him (and his judgment) the balance of the insurance money. That this scene takes place at a dance given by George Murchison's fraternity and attended by Walter and Ruth stretches credibility, since such behavior seems totally out of character for Walter. However, it does suggest some of the bourgeois pretensions implicit in Walter's desires and foreshadows the disappointment to come.

In another significant foray outside the Younger apartment, the family visits the new house and neighborhood into which they plan to move. Although a similar trip was included in the 1961 film, Hansberry's original directions included a panning shot of the surrounding houses which revealed "something sinister. . . . At some windows curtains drop quickly back into place as though those who are watching do not want to be seen; at others—shadowy figures simply move back out of view when they feel that Walter and Ruth's gaze is upon them; at still others, those who are staring do so without apology. The faces, the eyes of women and children, in the main, look hard with a curiosity that, for the most part, is clearly hostile." This brief visual moment emphasizes the dangers awaiting the Youngers in their new neighborhood and the courage of their decision to move.

By taking the camera outside the Younger apartment in her script and following the adult characters in their normal daily lives, Hansberry forces her audience to see the conditions and circumstances that drive a man like Walter to strike out at his family, that motivated Walter's father to quite literally work himself to death, that led Ruth to risk abortion rather than add another child to the family, and that impel a Lena Younger to move into a hostile neighborhood. The camera's eye would be irrefutable as it swept the panorama of Chicago and, by implication, America's major cities where the majority of African Americans reside.

Hansberry also accomplishes something else which the structure of the stage play and the 1961 film version could not—revealing the many subtle ways in which racism invades the characters' lives on a daily basis. The early scene with Mrs. Holiday, the woman for whom Lena works, is a case in point. It is a fascinating study in the complexities of the relationship between domestic and employer. On the one hand, Lena is gentle, though lovingly gruff and demanding, with the Holiday child on this, her last day before retirement. When Mrs. Holiday questions by mere tone of voice whether Lena can really say good-bye to the child—suggesting in that moment the historic myth that mammies surely prefer their white charges over their own families—Lena curtly affirms that the good-bye is indeed a final one.

Lena remains unmoved even when Mrs. Holiday indicates that her leaving will cause some "hardship" for the family, since she will probably have to stop working until she can find a suitable replacement. When Mrs. Holiday finally accepts the inevitable, Lena relaxes and speaks in a more friendly and intimate tone, telling her about her work history, first for a woman who considered her "part of the family" and used that as an excuse to severely underpay her, and later Lena's failed attempt to retrain for employment in the defense industry. She speaks with pride of her husband, who mastered the new demands of defense employment and left his porter job for good. This dimension of Lena, who could easily be portrayed as a stereotypical mammy if not handled with sensitivity, allows the viewer to understand her insistence on certain values and the significance of the insurance money to her and her family. Without this scene, we fail to comprehend fully Lena Younger and the years of Mrs. Holidays and worse that she has lived through. Scenes like this lend texture to the lives of the Younger family.

Why were such important scenes cut from the film that was made? In my opinion, the editing of Hansberry's film script was implicitly political and began with the editorial notes of production director Samuel Briskin (secured sometime later by Robert Nemiroff, Hansberry's literary executor). It is a measure of the cultural ignorance of the times that Briskin registered confusion at the pet names used by the family—that Beneatha was called "Bennie," and Walter Lee "Brother." "Jive" expressions, such as "Man," "I mean," and "like," were deleted as much as possible.

These and other colloquialisms were essentially purged from the script.

Other comments and recommendations were more insidious, such as deleting the white clerk who was fresh to Lena in the market, cutting the scene in Herman's liquor store after registering a failure to understand why Walter gets angry at the store owner, questioning the play's explicit references to colonialism perpetrated by the British and the French, and questioning the advisability of most racial references such as "white boys." Also cut from the script was a brief reference to the quality of Travis's school. His teacher asks him and his classmates to bring fifty cents for a fund to buy special books "that tell all about the things the poor Negroes did." The issue of teaching "Negro history" as something different and apart (probably during a one-week "celebration") and the teacher's constant reference to "poor Negroes" get lost in the more urgent money problems of the family. But the comments quickly remind us that quality of education is another reason that families like the Youngers move to other neighborhoods.

Briskin circled "white— black—" in Asagai's speech referring to the white and black women that he had known and probably dated. Beneatha's blasphemous speech about God raised the question, "Are we apt to get church criticism on this?" And, in an amusing example of illiteracy, Briskin suggested that Beneatha's speech to George about the "Ashanti performing surgical operations when the British were still tattooing themselves with blue dragons" be replaced by suggesting that the "Americans were doing something or other." Obviously, at that time, the only Americans were Native Americans.

Briskin speaks with the voice and authority of the movie studios (Columbia in this instance), who were incredibly cautious about offending the American (i.e., white) public. This timidity is most evident in the deletion of Hansberry's new scenes depicting encounters with whites, in particular, Lena's scene with Mrs. Holiday and Walter's meeting with the liquor store owner. Neither white character is blatantly racist, but rather displays that persistent insensitivity and often willful blindness that cuts as deeply as, but less conspicuously than, legal segregation. The subtle racism of the North is Hansberry's target. These characters are not the "white other," the Southern bigot whose outrageous actions are easily distanced, but resemble more closely probably those whom the studio hoped to attract to the film. Only the scenes with Lindner, message-carrier for the Clyborne Park Association, were retained. Tested in the highly successful stage production, they were clearly regarded as safe.

The fear of what Hollywood would do with her film had made Hansberry very reluctant to sell the movie rights. "My twenty years of memory of Hollywood treatment of 'Negro materials,' " she wrote in her newspaper article, "plus the more commonly decried aspects of Hollywood tradition, led me to visualize slit skirts and rolling eyeballs, with the latest nightclub singer playing the family's college daughter. I did not feel it was my right or duty to help present the American public with yet another later-day [sic] minstrel show." Yet despite the ignorance and timidity expressed by the production director, Hansberry apparently felt that the final script met her high standard for socially responsible art, and retained the essential spirit, dignity, and quality of the original play which, she said, had gone up on Broadway "without a single line having been changed for the 'buyers' or anyone else."

Daniel Petrie, director of the 1961 film, was not so sanguine about the results after seeing his work at the Cannes Film Festival. He was quite disappointed with the European reception of the film, which received a special Gary Cooper Award for "human values" but was bypassed for Cannes' regular prizes. "Objections to *A Raisin in the Sun* . . . mentioned the excessive dialogue—all too literally translated in three-layer subtitles—and the confinement of the action to the stage set without moving outdoors. Also, while the theme was liked, there was so little visual emphasis on the poor living conditions of the Chicago Negro family that foreign audiences didn't see what they had to complain about."*

Petrie concluded that the final cutting of the film was at fault. The exterior scenes in the original screenplay, which were filmed on location in Chicago and visually depicted the crucial housing problems of the city, extended the length of the film to two hours and forty minutes. "To shorten it," commented Petrie, "most of the visual description of the neighborhood was removed, while almost all of the play's dialogue remained. When I saw the foreign audience grow restless, I was convinced that the wrong things had been cut out." Hansberry's initial cinematic instincts were on the mark. Her exterior scenes, which included the family's encounters with the dominant and oppressive culture, documented the conditions that drove the characters in her play and provided the context for any audience to understand the dilemma and frustration of the Younger family.

In the original film script, Hansberry may have attempted to correct what she considered to be a flaw in the stage drama. She wrote: "Fine plays tend to utilize one big fat character who runs right through the middle of the structure, by action or implication, with whom we rise or fall. A central character as such is certainly lacking from *Raisin*. . . . The result is that neither Walter Lee nor Mama Younger loom [sic] large enough to monumentally command the play. I consider it an enormous dramatic fault if no one else does. . . ."** This dual protagonist structure set the stage for the struggle for primacy between actors Sidney Poitier and Claudia McNeil in the 1959 Broadway production. The audience's recognition of the matriarchal

*Eugene Archer, " 'Raisin' Director Plans Two Films, *New York Times*, June 10, 1961, p. 12.
**"Willie Loman, Walter Younger, and He Who Must Live," *Village Voice*, August 12, 1959, p. 8.

figure as portrayed by a powerful McNeil and the culturally conditioned fear of the volatile Walter tended to award the victory to Lena.

Without making major revisions in the play for her screenplay, Hansberry subtly tilts the balance toward Walter Lee from Lena Younger by emphasizing Walter's role as a representative of African American men. She drops the warrior scene in which Beneatha and Walter dance to African rhythms and Walter, in a drunken speech to his "African brothers," speaks in another, more subliminal voice as he momentarily identifies with the proud, militant heritage of his forebears. That moment was delightful to those who viewed it as innocent play, but was problematic for others. It seemed completely out of character for Walter, who constantly denigrates Beneatha's identification with Africa. Because of Walter's drunken state, his speech tends to undercut any serious notions of brotherhood among people of African descent. Whatever the interpretation, Hansberry achieves much more with the street orator who, speaking for Walter, connects unequivocally the struggle of African Americans to that of Africans with very explicit and compelling arguments. Hansberry insists that the crowd at the street meeting be primarily male, thereby emphasizing the particularly insidious effects of racism and discrimination on the African American male. Bringing gender into the foreground in this way helps to frame Walter's sexist remarks about the women in his family who "man the barricades," who have "small minds," and who generally prevent him (and men like him) from taking the bold actions he believes are necessary to be successful in this country.

Hansberry also clarifies the motivation for Walter's decision to reject Lindner's offer in the final moments of the film. There has been much debate as to the reasons for his change of heart. Is it the overpowering presence and pressure of his mother, who insists that his son be present, that shames Walter into changing his mind? Or is it something inside Walter that insists on the more prideful choice? The answer determines Walter's stature as either a man dragged kicking and screaming into his mother's definition of manhood or a man who is capable of a courageous and rather stunning act of self-realization. Hansberry leaves no doubt as to her intentions.

> WALTER: What's the matter with you all? I didn't make this world! It was give to me this way! Hell yes (*to his sister*) I want me some yachts someday! Yes, I want to hang some real pearls round my wife's neck! Ain't she supposed to wear no pearls? Somebody tell me *who* it is who decides which women is supposed to wear pearls in this world? I tell you, I am a *man*—and I think my wife should wear some pearls in this world!

. . . The last line hangs and Walter begins to move about the room with enormous agitation, as if the word "man" has set off its own reaction in his mind. He mumbles it to himself as he moves about. **The interplay of his conflict is at work now in him, no matter what he says. It is the realization that begins now that will decide his actions to come; thus he is quarreling with Walter Lee; all actions he performs are to persuade himself.** [Emphasis added]

Finally, Hansberry makes a subtle but telling change in the ending of the screenplay. In the original drama, Mama is left alone on the stage, after the family members have exited with the last of their belongings.

For a long, long moment, she looks around and up and out at all the walls and ceilings, crosses Upstage Right to what was once her and Big Walter's bedroom, touches the door jamb, crosses Centerstage and suddenly, despite her, a great heaving thing rises in her and she puts her fist to her mouth to stifle it, takes a final desperate look, pulls her coat about her, pats her hat and exits.—The lights come down even more—and she comes back in, grabs her plant, and goes out for the last time. Lights down and out.

FINAL CURTAIN*

In contrast, the screenplay ends with *both* Walter and Lena in the frame.

> WALTER: (*gently*) Mama, why don't you come on!
> LENA: I'm coming, I'm coming.
> WALTER: (*grinning to relieve the moment*) Mama, how we gonna pay for this house?
> LENA: Well, I was just thinking the other day that I didn't like not working much as I thought I did. . . . I guess I call Mrs. Holiday in the morning—see if they got somebody else yet. . . .

They suddenly look at each other in a flash of remembrance, and Walter turns and goes to the window and gets the plant and comes back and puts it in his mother's hands, and they go out and down the steps—their conversation about the nature of the future going on: Walter suggesting that Charlie Atkins might someday want a partner if he can get the capital together. . . .

FADE OUT

Both endings are preceded by the comments by Lena and Ruth that Walter has come into his manhood, but the latter scene emphasizes Walter's new role in the family as co-leader with his mother. The plant, which "expresses" Lena, remains a critical symbol here. It embodies her hopes, dreams and values. The fact that Lena *and* Walter suddenly "remember" it and that Walter places the plant in her hands is poignant affirmation that Walter has indeed accepted those human principles that have seen his family

*Lorraine Hansberry, *A Raisin in the Sun*, Thirtieth Anniversary Edition, Revised (New York: Samuel French, 1988), p. 134.

through generations of discrimination. At the same time, he represents a new generation of African Americans who will and must seek their future in the opportunities offered by their own times. In these post-feminist 1990s, such a change may achieve Hansberry's intention to emphasize the plight of Walter more effectively. In the earlier versions, Walter Lee often seems infantile in his actions, and his reactions read as tantrums in a world sensitized to feminist issues. Combined with the location shots that emphasize the economic and social traps surrounding him, this change in the ending grants him greater stature without sacrificing the central importance of Lena.

Although *A Raisin in the Sun* was the first and only one of her film scripts to be produced, Hansberry had thought and written for several years about Hollywood films and their treatment of African Americans. In an essay written ten years before her film, she wrote:

> What is it exactly that we Negroes want to see on the screen? The answer is simple—*reality*.
>
> We want to see films about a people who live and work like everybody else, but who currently must battle fierce oppression to do so.
>
> We want to see films about lynchings that *did* come off—or that *can be stopped* by the mass intervention of black and white all over the country. Or about job-hunting when you are black; or house-hunting or school-hunting; about restaurants, hotels, theatres that do not admit.
>
> We want an end to the evasions . . . so that all the world can see who our oppressors are and what lies at the root of their evil.
>
> And lastly, we want employment for our young writers and actors who can best give expression to our sorrow, songs and laughter, to our blues and our poetry—and the very drama of our lives.*

*"The Mystery of the Invisible Force: Images of the Negro in Hollywood Films," unpublished composite from articles written for the student magazine *New Foundations*, 1951.

Hansberry's original screenplay for *A Raisin in the Sun* meets her test for reality and offers eloquent testimony to her belief that art and social responsibility are synonymous.

COMMENTARY: THOUGHTS ON THE SCREENPLAY

by Spike Lee

History is an important word, an important concept, but today it seems like this particular word is foreign to a lot of us African Americans. The history I'm talking about is not ancient African history either; it's recent history. If you polled all the black players in the NBA, I'd bet my left arm only a couple could tell you who was the first black player in the league. The same with the NFL; a greater percentage would know about Jackie Robinson being the first in baseball, but there still might be some who didn't have a clue. (I choose these examples because I'm an avid sports fan, but the same results would be evident across the board. Young African American kids know the names of Martin Luther King, Jr., and Malcolm X, but it's a very superficial knowledge.) A lot of us are again clueless about Ms. Hansberry.

It's time to include Lorraine Hansberry in those history lessons. Reading her original screenplay of *A Raisin in the Sun* was a revelation for me. I had seen the movie on television, but I was too young to have seen the Broadway production (I would have probably liked it better than the film). Like all great works of art, this stuff doesn't get old. And for me *Raisin* is still fresh, it's still relevant. Lorraine Hansberry was a visionary.

Today, everybody and their mother are talking about
"Afrocentricity." But Hansberry was writing about it long
before it became fashionable. ("Hell no, don't call me no
African! I'm a Negro, I'm colored, etc., etc." We've all
heard that numerous times.) For me, the brilliance of *Raisin* is the examination of the African American family. And
we all have to ask ourselves, have things gotten any better
than when the play was written? I have to say I think
they've gotten worse. We've made some advances as a people, but our families have gotten weaker. Back in the day
when Lorraine wrote this play, we did not have the astro-
nomical amount of teenage mothers, the drugs, the black-
on-black crime, young black males dying at one another's
hands, the miseducation of black youth, and so on. This is
a big part of the reason why we're in the sorry state we're
in. The black family structure is at an all-time low.

But with this recent so-called "explosion" of black cin-
ema, the names most repeated are Oscar Micheaux, Gordon Parks, Ossie Davis, and Melvin Van Peebles. From
this day on, I'm going to start to include Ms. Hansberry.
Her play is a landmark in American theater, and in the
right hands, the film could have been a landmark in cin-
ema. (Regardless, it still stands as an important piece.)
One sees the freedom she had with the play that Hollywood, or in this specific case, Columbia Pictures, wasn't
having.

After I finished reading the screenplay, I went out and
rented the video cassette. It seems to me all the cuts had
to deal with softening a too defiant black voice. I found
the parts that were cut to be some of the most interesting
parts of the screenplay. Of course, Columbia probably
cited length as the reason for the deletions. But I feel Lorraine was right in her vision to "open up" the play. She
just didn't want to film a *play*; *she wanted to make it cinematic, to make it a film.* In the final result, the film is very
stagey. It's my guess that once she signed her deal, she had
very little say on how the project would be realized. And

it was a triumph for her to write the screenplay and get the film made.

You might ask, what would Hansberry have done if she hadn't been taken away from us so soon? I'd like to think that *Raisin* would have been her first of many fine screenplays. Can you name another African American female who has written a screenplay for a Hollywood studio that got made? I cannot.

The history must be taught, and if not in the schools then at home. But that won't or can't be done until our home life, our families, get back on track. It's a vicious cycle. We still have a long, long way to go.

A RAISIN
IN THE SUN

THE UNFILMED
ORIGINAL SCREENPLAY

FADE IN:

BEFORE TITLES

PANNING SHOT: EXT.—SOUTHSIDE CITY
LANDSCAPE; BACKYARDS, BOULE-
VARDS, KITCHENETTES, ETC.

IMPOSE: LANGSTON HUGHES'S POEM, SIN-
GLE LINE PER FRAME *(one line at a time)*
OVER PANNING SHOTS:

> What happens to a dream deferred?
> Does it dry up
> Like a raisin in the sun?
> Or fester like a sore—
> And then run?
> Does it stink like rotten meat?
> Or crust and sugar over—
> Like a syrupy sweet?
>
> Maybe it just sags
> Like a heavy load.
>
> *Or does it explode?*

FADE OUT:

TITLES

AFTER TITLES FADE, FADE IN:

EXT.—MEDIUM-SIZED APARTMENT BUILD-
ING. MEDIUM PANNING SHOT—EARLY
MORNING.

The unmistakable grating noise of an alarm clock intrudes as we move over the city-stained brick building.
It is old enough, for the Middle West, but it is not a
tenement. It would be a reasonable place to live but for
overcrowding. Its disease is not so much deterioration as
that it was built to accommodate roughly one-half the
people who now live in it.

PANNING SHOT CONTINUES UP OR DOWN
INTO THIRD-FLOOR APARTMENT
THROUGH TINY (I REPEAT, T-I-N-Y)
WINDOW.

Camera comes in freely and inspects this apartment
which is the home of the Younger family headed by the
widowed Lena Younger. Primarily we see that almost all
features of this home suffer from the multiplicity of uses
to which they are put daily.

Such are, for instance, that the living room never had an
opportunity to be only a living room. Once upon a time
it was the bedroom for Beneatha, the young daughter of
the family. At that time, her nephew Travis, who now
sleeps here, was obliged—from infancy to his ninth
year—to sleep behind a screen which Walter Lee, his
father, rigged in the bedroom he shared with Ruth, his
wife. It was an unhappy arrangement and the family was
bitterly antagonized by it for many years, but there
was no alternative to the child sharing the room with his

parents while his almost-grown aunt slept on the living room couch because, after all, her father was still alive. But now Big Walter is dead, and Beneatha has inherited the second bed in her mother's room, thus permitting Travis to move to the "privacy" of the living room's make-down bed after all eating, entertaining, and other amenities of family life have been completed of an evening.

This is the ghetto of Chicago. These people live here because rents in their ghetto are proportionately higher than in any other place in the city; therefore even slight improvement would be of a nature to exhaust them financially since the hard-earned combined wages of the three income-making members must feed, clothe, and house five people. Plus the fact that it is an ambitious family that has somehow (another story) managed to put one member through three years of college. Thus, they live here. Not indolence, not indifference, and certainly not the lack of ambition imprisons them, but various enormous questions of the social organization around them which they understand in part, but only in part.

By the same token, the kitchen is a little boxed-in area where oilcloth covers as many things as possible. It is clearly, to any fool, really only one room—but the landlord's lease is dramatically insistent on the fact that it constitutes "two rooms," and they pay accordingly. Care should be taken with the furnishings of this room. These people are expressed by what they have intentionally brought into this apartment and what things they are obliged to simply endure. They are not so much "poor" as working-class; therefore poverty, as such, has no place in this house. *They* would think of "poor" people as someone down the street to whom *they* contribute at Christmastime. Things are *worn* in this house, they are never ragged; things are overused, they are never *dirty*. If anything, the upholstery has been brushed and soused in various cleaning

fluids so often that their texture is slick and shiny—not oily
and soiled. And, to cover all, Mama has persistently pinned
on little ornate doilies wherever a head may touch or a
hand may lie. As for the tastes which are apparent: well,
they are many, different, but mainly the mother's. She was
born someplace in the border South about 1890 (she thinks;
nobody kept records of Negro children when she was born
down there, and she is very vague about the matter). She
may have gotten past the eighth grade, but it is unlikely.
Her own tastes, then, are culled from her memories of
things which seemed truly grand to her when she was a
girl: big, heavy pieces full of curls and carvings, and laces—
tablecloths and, sometimes, dresses. Someplace in this
crowded house she probably still has a cherished chest of
fabrics and objects which, from year to year, the sophisticated would variously laugh at or worship—depending on
their vogue. In later years her tastes have been molded by
a general American lower-class appreciation for the glossy.
The "paintings" reflect this. They are, in the main, unbe-
lievably stylized chromo reproductions of flamboyant pea-
cocks or winter sleigh-scenes and the like. The carpet is an
ancient Oriental affair; it was probably the most expensive
single item ever collected for this house, a long, long time
ago. She cannot abide the look of barrenness; thus the
clutter of their living is heightened by the collection of such
things as the artificial fruit in a truly grotesque frosted glass
bowl on the dining/living-room table and similar objects
d'horror all over the place, including on top of the coffee
table (which she allowed Ruth to pick, perhaps, and which
is a little more simple and "modernistic" for that reason)
and on top of the television set, which is huge and bald-
faced.

Occasionally, as with the coffee table, Ruth might have
affected the choice of this or that item. Beneatha's ten-
dency is to simply complain every now and then about "all
this junk." But her effort to change the actual character of

the apartment is meager and consists in the main of scattered random objects in the family living area and the bedroom she shares with Mama: cameras, maracas, parts of a human skeleton, phonograph records, books, etc., which attest to her often fleeting interests.

During the day the place is inclined to darkness, because the little window (except for one each in the bedrooms) is the only window in the apartment and it draws its light from between a shaftway which permits very little, and that only during the early day. It is here that Mama has chosen to hopefully grow a small and miserable-looking plant, in which her imagination, alone in the universe, has invested a spirit of heroism.

The camera lingers a moment on the plant as it pans in, and then goes on to study the apartment before:

STATIONARY SHOT—MED.—RUTH

RUTH *is standing at the stove, visibly in physical discomfort; her eyes closed momentarily as if she is waiting for a spasm of some kind to pass. The ringing continues—from another part of the house. The spell passes. She steadies and looks with annoyance toward her bedroom, where her husband is still sleeping. The make-down bed in the living room, side-angled, background, is tossed asunder, marking the fact that someone has arisen from it. The ringing continues as she clangs the pots and keeps looking at her bedroom with anger.*

CLOSE SHOT—RUTH

RUTH: Now you know if I can hear it out here then you can! *(She listens for a stir of life, and then:)* Man, if you don't get up . . . *(She listens.)* All right—you just go ahead and lie there, and the next thing you know Travis'll be out and Mr. Johnson'll be in there and you'll be fussing and cussing round here like a madman and be late, too. *(She waits.)* Walter Lee—it is time for you to get up! *(She waits; at the end of her patience she starts toward the room.)*

MED. TRACKING SHOT WITH RUTH TO BEDROOM—

Walking as an angry and determined woman walks.

INT.—MED. CLOSE—BEDROOM—DARK— WALTER IN BED—P.O.V.: RUTH

WALTER *turns over on his back slowly, very much awake. He lifts one hand and lets it fall listlessly to the bed to signify to his wife that he is awake.*

GENERAL SCENE—TO INCLUDE RUTH

She sees gesture, sighs, angrily steps to dresser where clock is and snaps it off and walks out of room.

CLOSE SHOT—WALTER

He fumbles under his pillow and produces a cigarette, which he lights. He reaches out one hand and lets up the shade, which is so close in the small room that he does not have to rise in the bed to do so. The light which comes in this window is also interrupted as if another structure intercepts part of it and perhaps throws a distinctive shadow into the scene. Offscreen his wife's voice calls him once again—in final irritation. He rises.

LONG SHOT—WALTER LEANING IN DOORWAY TO ROOM—P.O.V.: RUTH.

WALTER LEE YOUNGER *is in his mid-thirties. His mismatched and rumpled pajamas cover a taut lithe body charged even at this morning awakening hour with a perceptible intensity emanating outward as a "presence." His face is not so much handsome as concentrated. Something in this man's world must be made to work for* him *and those he loves; we can be sure of this.*

> WALTER: When the bell rings . . . get up. When the bell rings . . . get the car. What would happen if there wasn't no more bells?

QUICK CLOSE FLASH— RUTH AT STOVE

> RUTH: Why you always got to smoke before you eat in the morning?

GENERAL SCENE—FULL SHOT

> WALTER *(finding his watch on coffee table and strapping it on)*: Is he out yet?

> RUTH: What you mean, *out*? He ain't hardly had a chance to be in there good yet.

> WALTER: Well, what you doing all that yellin' for if I can't even get in there!

RUTH *puts down her spoon with definition and turns to him.*

> RUTH: Listen, Walter, please, don't get up and start fighting with me on your mother's very first day home.

> WALTER *(slapping his head with realization)*: The check's coming today?

RUTH: Well, they promised Saturday and this *is* just Friday. And I hope you sure ain't going to get up first thing today talkin' 'bout no money 'cause I 'bout don't want to hear it. What kind of eggs you want?

WALTER: Not scrambled.

She immediately begins to absentmindedly beat the daylights out of the eggs; he does not bother to protest, merely notes it with a hopeless glance.

Where's the paper?

RUTH: On the table in front of you. *(Dully:)* If it was a snake it would of bit you.

WALTER *(she is getting to him)*: Oh, you are just one happy little woman, ain't you! *(Reading the front-page news of the day:)* Says Colonel McCormick is sick.

RUTH: Is he now? Poor thing.

WALTER *(consulting his watch)*: What in the name of God is that boy doing in there? He's just gonna have to start getting up earlier mornings. I can't be being late to work on account of him playin' around in there.

MED. CLOSE—RUTH *as she wheels—*

RUTH *(a burst of passion)*: Oh no, he ain't going to be gettin' up one second earlier mornin's. It ain't his fault that he can't get to bed no earlier nights cause his father got a collection of good-for-nothing loudmouths sitting up running their mouths in what is *supposed* to be his bedroom after ten o'clock at night!

MED.—WALTER

WALTER: Un-hunh. That's what you mad about, ain't it? The things I got to talk about with my friends just couldn't be important in your mind, could they!

GENERAL SCENE

RUTH (*under breath, turning back to her work*): Such friends as you got . . .

WALTER *rises and walks over to the window, which is right behind where she is trying to prepare breakfast at the stove; thus, this also annoys her, but she suppresses complaint.*

EXT.—SLANTED SHOT TO SIDEWALK—DAY—P.O.V.: WALTER

A few Southsiders, hunched against Chicago autumn early-morning chill, run to catch u bus.

INT.—CLOSE-UP—WALTER'S FACE *watching them*

WALTER: Just look at 'em . . . running and racing to work. All the little bells makin' 'em run . . .

WIDER ANGLE TO INCLUDE RUTH

He turns to study her; for the first time a playful smile breaks on his lips.

WALTER: You look young this morning, baby.

*In character, she shrugs with indifference. Still feeling sud-
denly mellow, he reaches out playfully to catch her about
the waist as she comes near him to get something from the
stove.*

> Look just like you did when I was courtin' you.
> When you was stirrin' them eggs just now—

*She pulls away from him roughly, and his expression
changes accordingly.*

> It's gone now, though. You look just like your-
> self again.

GENERAL SCENE—FULL SHOT—LIVING ROOM-
KITCHEN *which includes door to outside hall which leads
to, among other things, the community bathroom of the
floor.* TRAVIS *appears, half-dressed, and signals his father
to run out to the bathroom in a hurry.* WALTER *grabs his
towels, etc., and runs out.*

INT.—HALLWAY—WALTER—NEIGHBOR

At the bathroom WALTER *almost physically collides with*
MRS. JOHNSON, *a slightly built woman who has rushed
equi-distance from her apartment determined to prevail.*
WALTER *gets his hand on the bathroom knob first and slides
in past his neighbor who throws up her hands in frustration,
backs off and gives a vociferous look at the slammed door.
We are left with the impression that we will see this feisty
woman, about Lena Younger's age, again.*

*[This is the only major change made in this script. Inconsis-
tently, Hansberry injected the character of Mr. Johnson,
who was never thereafter seen in the play. His wife, on the
other hand, later provides a significant counterpoint to Lena
Younger in a major scene establishing her own character*

*juxtaposed against that of Lena's to specifically illustrate
Hansberry's concern that the seemingly traditional head of
the Younger household be seen as a rebel in her own right.
Mr. Johnson is therefore eliminated here so as to provide
introductory context for Mrs. Johnson.*]

INT.—LIVING ROOM–KITCHEN—TRAVIS, RUTH—FULL SHOT

TRAVIS *at ten is a sturdy little boy inclined to a crisply
intelligent if boyish manner. His mother is a petite, pretty
woman who now wears already an expression of ingrained
fatigue. The boy pulls up a chair to the table in order to
have his breakfast, which she puts before him without a
word.*

> TRAVIS: Mama, this is Friday. *(Gleefully:)* Check
> coming tomorrow, huh?

> RUTH: You get your mind off money and eat
> your breakfast.

> TRAVIS: This is the morning I'm supposed to
> bring the fifty cents to school, Mama.

> RUTH: What fifty cents?

> TRAVIS: The fifty cents a month we supposed
> to bring from now on for the "poor Negroes in
> history."

CLOSE SHOT—RUTH *as this registers so early in the
morning.*

> RUTH: For who?

TWO SHOT

> TRAVIS: Teacher says we got to do something
> 'bout teaching colored kids 'bout their history.

So they set up a fund to buy special books that tell all about the things the poor Negroes did.

RUTH: Is that the way she told you about it? About the "poor Negroes"?

TRAVIS: Yes ma'am. She always says "the poor Negroes."

RUTH: How come there got to be *special* books?

TRAVIS *(painfully, exasperated with an adult)*: Because—I told you—it's about *Ne-groes*. About Negro history.

RUTH: How many different kinds of history they got over at that school where I am sending you? Seem like to me the man who writes the rest of the books ought to get around to writing the Negro part. Besides, I ain't got no fifty cents this morning.

TRAVIS: Aw, Mama.

RUTH: Eat your breakfast now, Travis.

TRAVIS: I am eating.

RUTH: Well, hush and just eat! I got too much on me this morning to be listening to all your foolishness.

TRAVIS: Maybe Daddy—

RUTH: I said *hush!*

He hushes, jabs his spoon angrily into his cereal bowl, and rests his head upon his fists in dejection.

GENERAL SCENE—FULL SHOT—LIVING ROOM—
RUTH, TRAVIS

TRAVIS: Could I maybe go carry groceries at the supermarket after school then?

RUTH *stops all other activity completely and turns slowly where she stands and gives him an ominous final look. There is utter silence for a second. Then:*

RUTH: If you through eating you can get over there and make your bed up.

He obeys stiffly and goes to the make-down bed and angrily and carelessly tosses the thing together. He then gets his cap and books and presents himself to her, still pouting fiercely.

TRAVIS: I'm gone.

TWO SHOT—RUTH, TRAVIS

RUTH *automatically looks up from the stove to inspect him.*

RUTH: You got your carfare and milk money?

TRAVIS *(sullenly)*: Yes ma'am.

RUTH: And no sweet rolls today, sir! Dr. McHugh say your teeth got enough holes in 'em to keep him busy the rest of his life. And that ain't my objective in life.

TRAVIS *(sighing from oppression)*: Yes ma'am.

WIDER ANGLE TO INCLUDE DOOR *toward which the boy moves, having finished inspection and instruction. She watches him. He moves stiffly, almost in a parody of adult masculine outrage.*

EXTREME CLOSE SHOT—RUTH

His posture amuses her and touches her, and the first touch of softness that we have seen breaks at the corners of her lips as she watches him. Then, playfulness openly invades her expression.

> RUTH *(mockingly; as she thinks he would say it)*: Oh, that woman makes me so mad sometimes I don't know what to do! *(She waits.)* Hmph! I wouldn't kiss that woman goodbye for nothing in this world. Not for nothing in this world.

LONG SHOT—WIDE-ANGLED TO INCLUDE TRAVIS

She stands, waiting for him to respond to the new mood. He turns slowly and faces her, trying with all his power to resist the grin which tries to show itself on his face. He is defeated when she suddenly holds out her arms to him. He goes to her, grudgingly at first, then swiftly.

TWO SHOT

She holds him close to her, with the unabashed display of deep affection that emotionally aloof people will sometimes allow themselves more readily than others. She smooths the hair about his face and studies him.

> RUTH *(sweetly)*: Now whose little old angry man is this I got me here?

> TRAVIS: Aw—gaalleee, Mama.

RUTH *(boxing his head ever so gently as she teases)*: "Aw, gaalleeeeee, Mama!" Get on out of here before you be late to school.

TRAVIS *(immediately, in the face of love)*: Mama, could I pul-leese go carry groceries?

RUTH *(trapped a little)*: Honey, it's starting to get so cold evenings.

GENERAL SCENE—FULL SHOT—RUTH, TRAVIS, WALTER

WALTER *enters from bathroom, almost fully dressed and completely awake. He promptly draws a make-believe gun from a make-believe holster and shoots it at his son, who replies with an identical synchronized gesture.*

WALTER *(moving about, finishing his dressing)*: What is it he wants to do?

RUTH: Go carry groceries at the supermarket after school.

TRAVIS *(to his father, innocently, eagerly)*: For the poor Negroes in—

RUTH *(quickly)*: Never mind, baby, we ain't going though all of that again this morning.

WALTER: *(with a magnanimous wave of the hand)*: Let him go. It's good for him to be business-minded.

TRAVIS: I *have* to. She won't gimme the fifty cents.

CLOSE SHOT—WALTER

WALTER: Why not?

CLOSE SHOT—RUTH

RUTH *(with her flavor)*: 'Cause we ain't got it!

GENERAL SCENE (SOME CLOSE ANGLES)

WALTER: What you tell the boy things like that for? Here, Son.

He reaches, a little grandly, into his pocket and comes up with a coin, which he hands, also a little grandly, to his son. The boy accepts the money happily. RUTH stares at both with undisguised anger.

TRAVIS: Thanks, Daddy!

WALTER *deliberately stares back at his wife and suddenly, with malicious afterthought, reaches once more into his pocket and comes up with a second coin.*

WALTER: In fact, here's another fifty cents. Buy yourself some fruit today—or take a taxicab to school or something!

The boy jumps up and clasps his father around the middle with his legs, and they face each other in mutual appreciation.

TRAVIS: Hot dog!

WALTER, *aware of the near-violence shimmering in RUTH's eyes, lets the boy down.*

WALTER: Get out of here to school now.

TRAVIS *gets down and shouts goodbye and exits—*

WALTER: That's my boy.

He shakes his head with appreciation of the fact. RUTH *looks at him without appreciation and turns back to her work.*

You know what I was thinkin' 'bout in the bathroom this morning?

RUTH *(curtly)*: No.

WALTER: How come you got to be so pleasant all the time!

RUTH: What is there to be pleasant about?

WALTER: Do you want to know what I was thinking 'bout or not? *(angrily)*

RUTH *(with a sigh)*: I know what you was thinkin' 'bout and I don't want to hear it again.

WALTER's *sister,* BENEATHA, *enters scene from the bedroom she shares with her mother. She is dressed in a bright red nightie, the collegiate rage, and, with her long hair standing up wildly, or in hideous curlers, is a "sight." The daughter of the Younger family is about twenty, as slim and intense as her brother. She is not as pretty as her sister-in-law, but her lean, almost intellectual face has an appealing underlying gentleness and vulnerability. Still almost blind with sleep, she parades wordlessly to the outside door leading to the collective bathroom and disappears.*

RUTH *and* WALTER *ignore her, and* WALTER *goes on mumbling. His sister immediately reappears, the bathroom being occupied.*

WALTER: I was thinkin' 'bout what me and Willy Harris was talkin' about last night—

BENEATHA *(Imperiously, condescending to speak in passing from another country)*: Willy Harris is a good-for-nothing loudmouth.

She disappears into her room and closes the door. WALTER *furiously turns his attention at first to the closed door.*

WALTER *(shouting at the door)*: Anybody who talks to me is a good-for-nothing loudmouth, ain't he! *(Turning to indicate Beneatha and Ruth alike:)* And what do you all know about who is a good-for-nothing loudmouth? Charlie Atkins was a good-for-nothing loudmouth, too, wasn't he? When he wanted me to go into the dry-cleaning business with him. And now—God, that boy is grossing himself one hundred thousand dollars a year! One hundred thousand a year! You still call him a loudmouth?

RUTH *(bitterly)*: Oh, Walter Lee . . . *(She folds her head on her arms over on the table.)*

WALTER *(rising and coming to her and standing over her)*: You tired, ain't you? Tired of everything. Me, the boy, the way we live—this beat-up hole—everything. Ain't you?

She doesn't look up or answer.

So tired—moaning and groaning all the time. But you wouldn't do nothing to help, would you? You couldn't be on my side that long for nothing, could you?

RUTH: Walter, please leave me alone.

WALTER: A man needs for a woman to back him up. . . .

RUTH: Walter, please leave me alone.

MED. CLOSE SHOT—WALTER

He sits down at the table and directs his wife's attention to notice what he is doing.

WALTER: Mama would listen to you. You know she listens to you more than me and Bennie. All you would have to do is just sit down with her when you're drinking your coffee one morning, see—and just sip your coffee, see, and act like what you saying ain't really that important to you. You say *(he shows her how with his cup and manner)*—well, you kind of been thinking 'bout that deal that Walter Lee is so interested in. 'Bout the store and all. Then, you sip some more coffee, and keep it cool—and the very next thing you know, she's listening to you and asking you questions—and when I come home—

TWO SHOT—WALTER, RUTH

RUTH: Walter, leave me alone. That ain't none of our money and I ain't going to be harassing your mama about it.

WALTER: Baby, this ain't no fly-by-night proposition. This is gonna be something for real. I mean, we figured it out, me and Willy and Bobo.

RUTH *(with distaste)*: Bobo?

WALTER: Yeah. *(Waving the protest down:)* Ah, honey, you can't underestimate a man like Bobo. I mean, he's had him some bad breaks but that's life. I mean, like, what I like about the cat is—he don't quit tryin', you know what I mean?

CLOSE FLASH—RUTH'S FACE

RUTH: Walter, why don't you go to work?

TWO SHOT

WALTER *(preoccuped)*: It's just the beginning. Just the beginning.

WIDER ANGLE SHOT TO INCLUDE RUTH *as she rises from the table, indifferent to his plea.*

WALTER: Why can't you at least listen to me? What it take for you to just listen to me?

RUTH *(without turning to face him)*: Don't shout at me, Walter.

WALTER: Then listen to me sometimes, for God's sake!

RUTH: Don't shout at me.

WALTER: All right. *(More quietly, then the old desperation afresh:)* All right. *(Swiftly, glancing from his wife to his mother's bedroom door:)* Honey—honey . . .

She turns and faces him.

. . . it would only cost seventy-five thousand dollars. We figure the initial investment to be 'bout thirty thousand dollars. That come to ten each. *(Rubbing his ear:)* 'Course there's the couple of hundred you kind of have to spread around so's you don't have to spend your life just waitin' for them to get your license approved. . . .

RUTH *(deliberately, coldly)*: You mean graft.

WALTER: Oh, Ruth. *(Frowning with distaste at the use of the word:)* Oh, honey, don't call it that. You see, there's a woman's way of looking at things. Baby, don't you know don't nothin' happen for you in this world less you pay *somebody* off.

RUTH: I see. *(Pause.)* Walter, leave me alone. *(Another pause; then:)* Eat your eggs, they gonna be cold.

WALTER: That's it. There you are. *(Raising his hands and letting them fall impotently to his thighs with an air of bitter futility:)* Man say to his woman: "I got me a dream." His woman say: "Eat your eggs." Man say: "I got to take hold of this here world, baby." And a woman will say: "Eat your eggs and go to work." Man say: "I got to change my life, I'm choking to death, baby!" And that woman say, so help me God!— "Your eggs is getting cold!"

RUTH: Walter, that ain't none of our money.

CLOSE-UP—WALTER LEE

WALTER: This morning I was lookin' in the mirror and thinking about it: I'm thirty-five years old; I been married eleven years and I got a boy who sleeps in the living room—and all I got to give him is stories 'bout how rich white people live.

RUTH (*not quite meaning to say it*): Eat your eggs, Walter.

WALTER: Damn my eggs! Damn all the eggs that ever was!

GENERAL SCENE—FULL SHOT

BENEATHA *enters from bedroom and goes out to bathroom as before.*

RUTH: Then go to work.

WALTER: See—I'm trying to talk to you 'bout myself—and all you can say is "Eat them eggs" and "Go to work."

RUTH (*wearily*): Honey, you never say nothing new. I listen to you every day, and every night and every morning, and you never say nothing new. So you would rather *be* Mr. Arnold than his chauffeur. So—I would *rather* be living in Buckingham Palace.

WALTER: That is just what is wrong with women in this world. . . . Don't understand about building their man up and making them feel like they somebody. Like they can do something.

RUTH (*drily, but to hurt*): There *are* some men who do things.

WALTER: No thanks to their women.

BENEATHA *enters from bathroom.*

BENEATHA: I am going to start timing those people.

WALTER: You should get up earlier.

BENEATHA: Really—would you suggest dawn? Where's the paper?

WALTER *(pushing paper across the table to her as he studies her almost clinically)*: You a horrible-looking chick at this hour.

BENEATHA *(drily)*: Good morning, everybody.

WALTER *(senselessly)*: How is school coming?

BENEATHA: Lovely. Lovely. And you know, biology is the greatest. *(Looking up at him:)* I dissected something that looked just like you yesterday.

WALTER: I just wondered if you've made up your mind and everything.

BENEATHA *(gaining in sharpness and impatience)*: And what did I answer yesterday morning—and the day before that?

RUTH *(from the ironing board, like someone disinterested and old)*: Don't be so nasty, Bennie.

BENEATHA: And the day before that and the day before that!

WALTER *(defensively)*: I'm interested in you.

Something wrong with that? Ain't many girls who
decide—

WALTER and BENEATHA *(in unison)*: —to be a
doctor.

Silence.

WALTER: Have we figured out yet just exactly
how much medical school is going to cost?

RUTH: Walter Lee, why don't you leave that girl
alone and get out of here to work?

BENEATHA *(exits to bathroom and bangs on the
door)*: Come out of there, please!

She comes back into room.

WALTER: You know the check is coming
tomorrow.

BENEATHA *(sharpness itself)*: That money belongs to Mama, Walter, and it's for her to decide
how she wants to use it. I don't care if she wants
to buy a house or a rocket ship or just nail it up
somewhere and look at it. It's hers. Not ours—
hers.

WALTER *(bitterly)*: Now ain't that fine! You just
got your mother's interest at heart, ain't you,
girl? You just a nice girl—but if Mama got that
money she can always take a few thousand and
help you through school too—can't she?

BENEATHA: I have never asked anyone around
here to do anything for me!

WALTER: No! And the line between asking and just accepting when the time comes is big and wide—ain't it!

BENEATHA *(with fury)*: What do you want from me, Brother—that I quit school or just drop dead, which!?

WALTER: I don't want nothing but for you to stop acting holy round here. Me and Ruth done made some sacrifices for you—why can't you do something for the family?

RUTH: Walter, don't be dragging me in it.

WALTER: You are in it! Don't you get up and work in somebody's kitchen for the last three years to help put clothes on her back?

RUTH: Oh, Walter—that's not fair. . . .

WALTER: It ain't that nobody expects you to get on your knees and say "Thank you, Brother"; "Thank you, Ruth"; "Thank you, Mama"—and "Thank you, Travis, for wearing the same pair of shoes for two semesters"—

BENEATHA *(dropping to her knees)*: Well—I *do*—all right?—thank everybody. . . . And forgive me for ever wanting to be anything at all . . . forgive me, forgive me!

RUTH: Please stop it! Your mama'll hear you.

WALTER: Who the hell told you you had to be a doctor? If you so crazy 'bout messing round with sick people, then go be a nurse like other women—or just get married and be quiet. . . .

BENEATHA: Well—you finally got it said. . . . It took you three years but you finally got it said. Walter, give up—leave me alone. It's Mama's money.

WALTER: *He was my father, too!*

BENEATHA: So what? He was mine, too—and Travis's grandfather—but the insurance money belongs to Mama. Picking on me is not going to make her give it to you to invest in any liquor stores— *(under her breath)* and I for one say God bless Mama for that!

WALTER *(to* RUTH*)*: See—did you hear? Did you hear!

RUTH: Honey, please go to work.

WALTER: Nobody in this house is ever going to understand me.

BENEATHA: Because you're a nut.

WALTER: Who's a nut?

BENEATHA: You—you are a nut. Thee is mad, boy.

WALTER *(looking at his wife and his sister from the door, very sadly)*: The world's most backward nation of women, and that's a fact.

BENEATHA *(turning slowly in her chair)*: And then there are all those prophets who would lead us out of the wilderness—

WALTER *slams out of the house.*

—into the swamps!

RUTH: Bennie, why you always got to be pickin'
on your brother? Can't you be a little sweeter
sometimes?

Door opens. WALTER *walks in sheepishly.*

WALTER *(to* RUTH*):* I need some money for
carfare.

RUTH *(looks at him, then warms; teasing, but ten-
derly):* Fifty cents? *(She goes to her bag and gets
money.)* Here, take a taxi.

WALTER *exits as* RUTH *and* BENEATHA *giggle.*

LENA YOUNGER—*Mama—enters from her bedroom. She is
a woman in her early sixties, full-bodied and strong. She is
one of those women of a certain grace and beauty who wear
it so unobtrusively that it takes a while to notice. Her dark-
brown face is surrounded by the total whiteness of her hair,
and being a woman who has adjusted to many things in life
and overcome many more, her face is full of strength. She
has, we can see, wit and faith of a kind that keeps her eyes
lit and full of interest and expectancy. She is, in a word, a
beautiful woman.*

MED. CLOSE—LENA

LENA: Who that 'round here slamming doors at
this hour?

*She crosses through the room, goes to the window, opens
it.*

CLOSE-UP—PLANT IN WINDOW

A feeble little plant grows doggedly in a small pot. LENA's *hands enter frame. They feel the dirt, pack it down.*

RUTH *(offscreen)*: That was Walter Lee. He and Bennie was at it again.

MED. CLOSE—LENA

LENA: My children and they tempers. Lord, if this little old plant don't get more sun than it's been getting it ain't never going to see spring again.

FULL SHOT—GENERAL SCENE

LENA *(turning from the window)*: What's the matter with you this morning, Ruth? You looks right peaked. Bennie honey, it's too draughty for you to be sitting round half-dressed. Where's your robe?

BENEATHA: In the cleaners.

LENA: Well, go get mine and put it on.

BENEATHA: I'm not cold, Mama, honest.

LENA: I know—but you so thin. . . .

BENEATHA *(irritably)*: Mama, I'm not cold.

LENA *(seeing the make-down bed as* TRAVIS *has left it)*: Lord have mercy, look at that poor bed! Bless his heart—he tries, don't he?

LENA *moves to the bed* TRAVIS *has sloppily made up.*

RUTH: No—he don't half try at all, 'cause he knows you going to come along behind him and fix everything. That's just how come he don't know how to do nothing right now—you done spoiled that boy so.

LENA: Well—he's a little boy. Ain't supposed to know 'bout housekeeping.

EXTREME CLOSE SHOT OF LENA'S HANDS FIXING BEDDING

The camera inspects the hands carefully in this and the following shot. They are the hands of an older woman which have, however, only recently begun to show the fact of their age at all. The flesh is still tight and shiny on the bones. They are still rather strong hands.

LENA: My baby, that's what he is.

SLOW DISSOLVE TO:

INT.—EXTREME CLOSE-UP OF LENA'S HANDS WORKING AT BUTTONS ON A COAT—DAY

The camera continues to inspect the hands.

TWO SHOT: LENA AND SMALL WHITE CHILD

The CHILD, a girl, is about six or seven. LENA is somewhat impatiently buttoning up the coat of the little girl. It requires of her a certain awkward arrangement of the head and squinching of the eyes and a general, if slight, bending of some discomfort. They are in a child's bedroom of a nonluxurious but tastefully furnished modern apartment,

the home of a middle-income young white couple, the
Holidays.

CAMERA MOVES BACK TO SHOW:

WIDER ANGLE TO INCLUDE IMMEDIATE
BACKGROUND BEHIND LENA where a child's
school satchel and an apple lie waiting on a dresser.

> CHILD: Do you like apples?

LENA *replies to her with the neither kind nor unkind indifference of an adult who is otherwise preoccupied.*

> LENA: Uh-hunh.

TWO SHOT *as* LENA *finishes the buttoning and straightens
up, exhaling a little with relief to finish, and touching lightly
at the hips where the bending has most made itself felt. She
hangs the satchel on the* CHILD's *shoulder and hands her
the apple.*

> CHILD *(with childish and earnest irrelevancy)*: I
> love apples.

MED. CLOSE SHOT OF LENA'S UPPER BREADTH
AND FACE—P.O.V.: CHILD

*Shot catches the off-guard expression of a woman who, de-
spite her traditional gruffness with them, is easily and thoroughly charmed by small children. Her way with the girl is
that of one who knows perfectly how to play with small
people.*

> LENA: Is that so? Turn around so I can see you.

MED. CLOSE—TWO SHOT

The CHILD *makes a circle and ends up so as to face the* *woman again. They face each other in a little moment of* *quiet. Then:*

> *(folding her hands in front of her)* You gonna miss me?

The CHILD *stretches out her arms and clasps the woman about the middle.*

> CHILD: Oh, yes!

WIDER-ANGLED SHOT—HIGH—INCLUDING MORE OF ROOM'S BACKGROUND

LENA *bends and warmly receives and returns the embrace, then pushes the little girl back and inspects her hair and pats it a little with a brush, as they have mussed it in the embrace. The little girl starts to bite into her apple, and* LENA *matter-of-factly interrupts the action and takes her by the hand.*

> LENA: You save that for lunch time like I told you. Come on, now, and say goodbye to your Mama.

MED. TRAVELING SHOT FOLLOWS THEM OUT OF BEDROOM through living room of the apartment, which lies in a morning quiet and darkness, to kitchen door, which LENA pushes open.

LONG SHOT OF MRS. HOLIDAY FROM DOOR— P.O.V.: LENA

The girl's mother, MRS. HOLIDAY, *is sitting at the kitchen table in early-morning disorder. She has thrown a housecoat over her nightgown, and her hair has not yet been combed. She sits quietly, reflectively drinking her coffee. She is a youngish thirty or so, reasonably attractive. She looks up at them and smiles.*

FULL SHOT—GROUP

MRS. HOLIDAY: You all ready now, honey?

The little girl drops LENA's *hand and runs to her mother and puts her arms around her neck, and the mother returns the warm hug.*

MRS. HOLIDAY: You're going to be a very good
girl today, aren't you, sweet?

She pats the child once on her rear as LENA *comes and takes the child by the hand and leads her out of the kitchen. We stay with* MRS. HOLIDAY, *who goes on reflectively drinking her coffee. After a moment—about the length of time it would take* LENA *to walk the* CHILD *to the door of the apartment—*MRS. HOLIDAY *turns to watch* LENA's *re-entrance.*

MED. SHOT—LENA RETURNING THROUGH KITCHEN DOOR

Shot is low-angled to heighten the overtly determined and resolute set of LENA's jaw now that the two adults are alone. As she comes into the kitchen, her eyes deliberately avoid those of the other woman. She lets the kitchen door swing to with an air of finality and there is a

QUICK FLASH—MRS. HOLIDAY'S FACE *watching the older woman with far less certain intentions in her own face.*

GENERAL SCENE—LENA, MRS. HOLIDAY

LENA *moves briskly about the kitchen, putting away break-fast things. Then, in same spirit, she hauls a basket of about a half-dozen toys, of the stuffed, floppy, washable kind, from under the sink. She stops up the sink and begins to fill it with steaming hot water and adds soap powder to make lush suds.* MRS. HOLIDAY *watches, at first without comment. Then:*

MED. CLOSE SHOT—MRS. HOLIDAY

MRS. HOLIDAY: You don't need to bother with those crazy things on your last morning. I can send them out somewhere.

MED. CLOSE SHOT—LENA

Her jaw is set with stubbornness as she continues to wash a large, notoriously dirty, floppy rabbit. She scrubs his ears rather as if he were live and with much seriousness about the matter.

LENA: I ain't washing them for no reason but for her. I washed these things ever since I was here and I'll wash 'em before I leave. The Lord only knows what kind of strong disinfectant and mess they put in the water when they wash these things in them laundries. And half the time she still sticks 'em in her mouth at night the way she did when she was a baby. *(Lifting up another toy with disgust:)* Look at this rascal. Look just like he been crawling round in the coal room.

GENERAL SHOT (SOME CLOSE ANGLES ON DIALOGUE)

MRS. HOLIDAY *does not look at her employee, and there is a slight edge of pained disbelief in her voice when she speaks.*

MRS. HOLIDAY: You *really* told her goodbye?

LENA *(almost curtly)*: I 'spect we understood each other.

MRS. HOLIDAY: She's become so awfully attached.

LENA: She'll get over that. They always do. Part of growin' up.

CLOSE SHOT—LENA IN FOREGROUND AT SINK— HIGH ANGLE TO INCLUDE MRS. HOLIDAY IN BACKGROUND WATCHING HER

I called them catering people again 'bout the or-dures for your party Saturday night. Whether they ever gets here or not is something else. You better check on 'em.

MRS. HOLIDAY *(quietly from background)*: I will. Thank you.

LENA: That ought to be enough pie left over for tonight's supper—*if* your husband don't just have to have himself two slices. I cut off a little piece for the baby and put it in tin paper way at the back of the box so's that man wouldn't just eat it all up from her again.

MRS. HOLIDAY: All right. I'll remember.

CLOSE SHOT—MRS. HOLIDAY LOOKING DOWN AT HER CUP

I told Jerry last night. I held off telling him for a while. He was very upset. *(She tries a little*

smile.) You don't know how big a compliment
that is. Jerry is the one who always fired everybody else.

QUICK FLASH—LENA

Her jaw is set the same.

LENA *(almost curtly again)*: Well, thank him most
kindly for me.

CLOSE SHOT—MRS. HOLIDAY

MRS. HOLIDAY: We agreed that I would have to
quit the agency for a while. *(She runs her fingers
through her hair at the thought of it.)* I mean, you
never feel right about going off and leaving your
kid with—well—just anyone, the way some people do. *(She casts her eyes up quickly at Lena and
then down again.)* I'll just have to quit for a
while, that's all there is to it. *(There is a conspic-
uous silence for a few seconds, then:)* Jerry said
. . . Jerry said—that *(sucking in her breath)*
maybe if we got in someone else to do the washing and stuff . . .

ABRUPT MED. SHOT—LENA *as she absorbs the sense
of the remark and lifts her hands out of the water and shakes
them with strong, decisive movements that suggest her
exasperation.*

LENA: Mrs. Holiday—

MRS. HOLIDAY *(offscreen)*: Oh, I know. . . .

LENA: Mrs. Holiday—first of all, *I* am sixty-five
years old—

MRS. HOLIDAY: Yes.

LENA: —and second of all, you all can't afford no second person round here, and you ought to know it good as me.

Having made the pronouncement, she turns abruptly back to her washing.

EXTREME CLOSE-UP—MRS. HOLIDAY'S FACE *as* LENA *goes on talking.* MRS. HOLIDAY *closes her eyes and absorbs the truth with a slowly nodding movement of her head, and her expression finally changes to show that she has stopped resisting her own deep awareness of something she would rather, for personal interests, be able to argue against.* LENA's *voice continues offscreen as we stay with* MRS. HOLIDAY's *face.*

(persistent and talkative when she has caught hold of a subject): I am sixty-five years old and I *am* tired.

MRS. HOLIDAY: You won't believe me, but I said that to Jerry.

LENA: What?

MRS. HOLIDAY: Nothing. *(A gently embarrassed pause.)* I said that in spite of the hole it's going to leave us in for a while, I think it is very nice that you can finally stop working. *(She has said it in a rush, hoping to get it out without emotion.)*

LENA *(Resorting to gruffness to cover her own emotions in the face of the unexpected display of humanity)*: Hmph. I'm here to tell you it's nice! Somewhat long overdue, if anybody was to ever get around to asking me my opinion in the matter. Been working fifty-three years.

SLOW PANNING SHOT—CLOSE—P.O.V.: MRS. HOLIDAY

Shot begins with her eyes moving over the dishes in front of her on the kitchen table: a breakfast that has been prepared by LENA; across a sparkling linoleum floor which was washed by LENA; to a glistening refrigerator which was also washed by LENA, and a stove and a freezer and an entire assortment of kitchen appliances. They settle on a collection of symbolic but real brooms and mops and dust cloths and a pail sitting in a corner.

PANNING SHOT IS INTERPOSED WITH

(offscreen) Fifty-three years! Been working ever since I was twelve years old. Had to start too early and keep on too long . . .

PANNING SHOT LINGERS WITH BROOMS, ETC.— P.O.V.: MRS. HOLIDAY

Shot then pans down across the floor a short distance to LENA's feet clad in their black oxfords, in good repair, but inclined to tilt at the sides from weight. Pan slowly up the rock-of-Gibraltar legs, in heavy beige lisle stockings, to the dipping hemline which is peculiar to older women of large proportions; up the strong, still not stooping back, to the steel-gray hair caught with tidiness and rigidity in bun at the back of the head.

(still interposed): . . . and ain't none of it been what you could call fun, neither. I'll be most happy to carry this body home this afternoon and sit it down and let it rest, just let it rest—from here on in—and thank my husband's sweet memory for making it possible.

CLOSE SHOT—MRS. HOLIDAY

She is still absorbing and having a response to the quite unprovoked stream of conversation. Her eyes suggest that, like everyone else, she receives and reacts to it in her own context: in perhaps some personal way that has to do with her own life or a member of her family; or abstractly, with pure and simple human rapport. It is, for her, a moment of sympathy in depth, perhaps for the first time in her association with the older woman. We stay with her as LENA's *voice continues offscreen.*

I worked for one old woman when I was still a girl for twenty-two years. Twenty-two years! And one day at the end of them twenty-two, I went up to her and asked if she could see her way clear to pay me a little more. She'd like to had a heart attack right on the spot! *Twenty-two years*, mind you. Had practically raised her children for her, and all I was askin' for was a dollar and a half more, and she had the gall to stand there and look at me like I had hit her with something. She come drawing herself up to me in a state of clear shock and telling me *(a brutal, if accurate, mimic, harsh and shrill and reminiscent of the spirit if not the grammar of the incident)* "Why, *Lee-na*! I never thought to hear *you-ou* talk as if you thought of this as a *job*!"

MRS. HOLIDAY *smiles, gently, knowingly.*

"Why, we ain't never thought of you as nothing other than just another part of our family!" I just stood there and looked at that sister and thought to myself, "I don't know what kind of member of no family you have down on their knees scrubbing all them floors and washing all them sheets all these years." I quit right then and there.

MRS. HOLIDAY: I don't blame you. *(With an interest that a census report would never inspire:)* Have—have you done domestic work all your life?

LENA: Near 'bout. 'Cept—*(sudden rich laughter of remembrance)*— 'cept, Lord have mercy, when the war, praise God, come along a few years back. That sure changed things for a while. My husband had been a porter on the railroads all his life, and just as soon as we heard they had started taking colored in the de-fense plants and all, me and him both marched right on over and took the classes they was giving in the welding and all.

MRS. HOLIDAY *(with delight)*: Really?

LENA: Yes indeedy. I don't reckon nobody would spend their life being a domestic if there was something better they could get to do, child.

MRS. HOLIDAY *(with happy incredulity)*: You were a welder?

CLOSE-UP—LENA'S FACE

She giggles a little at the question, then sobers immediately; the reportorial mood is broken, and the arch acuteness of what actually happened intrudes in her features and her manner of telling as the camera inspects her face.

LENA: Well . . . no. . . . You see, we was already in our fifties by then. Oh, Big Walter, my husband, he done all right. I mean, that man was so determined that he wasn't never going to carry no kind of whisk broom again that he learned good. *(With gentle sadness:)* It was too late for me, though. You ever seen one of them things? Your hand really have to be right steady or you can burn a hole in everything in sight—including yourself. To tell the truth, that thing almost scared me near 'bout to death, spittin' and sputterin' fire all over the place. And then they had one thing there that I tried to learn to work that shook like it was crazy. All but shook my dentures out. I had to give up to that mess and get back to something I could manage. *(Shaking her head with delicate pride:)* Walter did it, though. . . . When the war was over he was almost halfway through his fifties but he had learned him a trade—and he was so proud, not to never have to be a porter no more. . . .

DESCENDING CLOSE SHOT DOWN LENA'S FACE over her now explicitly proud features; her ample bosom; the arms immersed in the white suds. The camera fixes on the hands, which have locked in a powerful wringing of one of the toys, so that the knuckles of the woman's hands glisten and show their enormous strength in the action of labor. The camera freezes on them.

He was always talkin' about how a man's hands wasn't meant to carry nobody's slop jars and make their beds and all. Always said they was meant to turn the earth with or make things. . . . Always hated the idea of being a servant. . . . And I got a boy at home—my son, Walter Lee— who is just like him . . . just like him!

The camera advances on her hands until they fill the frame for the

DISSOLVE TO:

EXTREME CLOSE SHOT—THE HANDS OF WALTER LEE YOUNGER BUTTONING UP HIS LIVERY—DAY

SUPERIMPOSE OVER WALTER'S HANDS: EXT. CHICAGO'S UPPER NORTH SHORE DRIVE— PANNING GENERAL SHOT—MORNING

Shot establishes lush atmosphere of homes of the district.

SUPERIMPOSE OVER WALTER'S HANDS: EXT.— WALTER'S EMPLOYER'S HOME—MORNING

Camera pans over beautifully attended lawn and carefully landscaped hedges to window of luxurious home.

SUPERIMPOSE OVER WALTER'S HANDS; INT.— CLOSE PANNING SHOT INTO THE DINING ROOM

Panning camera selects and studies excellent and expensive furnishings across length of room to where . . .

SUPERIMPOSE OVER WALTER'S HANDS: STATIONARY SHOT—LOW ANGLE

. . . a woman in a dressing gown, seated at the table, is talking to a friend on the telephone leisurely over breakfast about shopping, theater, husband, children, etc. We do not see her face—only her voice, her gown, her manicured hand, tastefully jeweled, establish her character.

SUPERIMPOSE OVER WALTER'S HANDS: CLOSE PANNING SHOT

Camera moves through more of house with selectivity to further establish affluence of owners.

SUPERIMPOSE OVER WALTER'S HANDS:
EXT. SHOT CONTINUES TO EXT. OF GARAGE

Woman's voice continues offscreen as the sound of a tinkling bell, unnaturally loud, breaks into scene.

Camera moves back to wider angle to include more of the uniform and WALTER's face staring concentratedly at himself in a mirror on a wall in front of him. Now his taut lean intensity is fully apparent. His face has all the components of beautifully composed sculpture. The energy of his nervous system rarely distorts the utter symmetry of his features; thus, the totality of the restlessness and intensity of his personality constantly surges in the only two possible outlets on his face: his eyes. And the camera notices them intently.

LONG SHOT ACROSS THE CONSPICUOUSLY
GLEAMING BLACK HOOD OF A LIMOUSINE
—EYE LEVEL—TO WALTER'S BACK

We are in the garage shed of an extremely affluent estate. The garage is itself more than fit for human habitation, being immaculate and well insulated and appointed with plumbing (for the help). It is white, like a hospital, and such mechanical instruments as are common to take care of a well-cared-for automobile hang in orderly rows about the place. WALTER buttons the last button and slips his visored cap on without taking his eyes off the image of himself.

CLOSE SHOT

WALTER adjusts the cap, still regarding himself with antagonistic and obsessive interest in the uniform and cap. Bell tinkles again.

HIGH WIDE-ANGLED SHOT—TO BELL

attached to overhead beam of garage. Camera returns as
WALTER snaps to himself and climbs into the car. He slams
the door roughly and starts to back it out of the garage as
the bell tinkles again on

DISSOLVE TO:

INT. OF LIMOUSINE—DAY

WALTER, in uniform, is driving with grim preoccupation.
His employer is behind him in rear seat. We do not see
the face of the employer, only details of a well-made suit
and hands drawing papers out of the briefcase poised on
his knees.

> EMPLOYER: . . . and then I will want to be at
> the Shipley Building at noon.

CLOSE SHOT—EMPLOYER'S HANDS MOVING
BACK CUFF TO LOOK AT WATCH

> WALTER (*offscreen*): Yes sir.

CUT TO:

EXT.—TOWERING CHICAGO OFFICE BUILDING—
HIGH ANGLE—DAY

Limousine pulls up; WALTER *gets out, opens door for employer, who disappears quickly into office building.* WAL-
TER *gets back into car.*

MED. CLOSE SHOT—WALTER IN CAR

*He sits behind wheel, reads newspaper for a few seconds,
puts it down with restless irritation, just sits.*

FULL SHOT

Another idle Negro chauffeur, with cap pushed back, hands in pockets, strolls over to pass the time of day.

TWO SHOT

CHAUFFEUR: Sox did all right, didn't they, man?

WALTER: I guess. Don't follow the game much, man.

CHAUEFFEUR: No? Well, the game ain't what it used to be nohow. What horsepower you carry?

WALTER *(irritably)*: I don't know, daddy. It runs.

The second CHAUFFEUR *is affronted by* WALTER's *hostility.*

CHAUFFEUR: Well, like, if you don't want to be bothered, man, why don't you just say so.

He adjusts his cap in anger and walks away abruptly. WALTER *looks after him with a flash of regret, then shrugs and looks sullenly up at the building.*

LONG SHOT—P.O.V.: WALTER—SKYSCRAPER

SUPERIMPOSED ON IMAGE OF BUILDING: WALTER

FADE OUT

FADE IN:

EXT.—UNIVERSITY CAMPUS—DAY

INT.—CAMPUS LOUNGE—GENERAL SCENE—DAY

The room is filled with the typical activity of a student lounge. Tastefully appointed room, carpeting, draperies, heavy portraits of founders and faculty. Here and there, clusters of students chatter amiably; others seemingly indulge in more heated discussions. Somewhere, someone on- or offscreen trippingly exercises a Chopin melody on a piano. Elsewhere, in a corner, a group of students cluster on the floor and on the arms of chairs around a young woman who plays the guitar in undisturbed counterpoint to the unnoticed piano. Here and there, coffee cups and books add to the decor and mood of the lounge. Heavy slabs of autumn sunlight fall into the room from the blinds.

MED. CLOSE SHOT—BENEATHA, ASAGAI

ASAGAI *is a young African student, postgraduate, of about twenty-five. He has an easy informality of manner.* BE-NEATHA *sits before him on the floor, her arms about her knees as he leans forward from his chair, gesturing us if leading a song.*

ASAGAI: OH—

BENEATHA *(imitatively)*: OH—

ASAGAI: BA—

BENEATHA: BA—

ASAGAI: MOO—

BENEATHA: MOO—

ASAGAI: SHAY!

BENEATHA: SHAY!

ASAGAI: There, you have it! Opegaday! Obamoshay!

BENEATHA: Opegaday! Obamoshay!

TWO SHOT

ASAGAI: Wonderful. You should major in languages instead of medicine.

BENEATHA: If I don't get some loot together I'm not going to be able to major in anything.

ASAGAI: Oh, I thought—

BENEATHA: That's my mother's money.

ASAGAI: Oh.

BENEATHA: What is my present?

ASAGAI: You'll just have to wait until you see it.

BENEATHA: Is it what I asked for?

ASAGAI (*smiling*): How many ways are there to ask the same question?

BENEATHA: Phooey!

ASAGAI: "Phooey!" I wonder why American petulance is so charming.

BENEATHA: I am not petulant!

ASAGAI (*mockingly*): "I am not petulant!" See.

BENEATHA: Why do you always make fun of me?

ASAGAI: Because you delight me.

BENEATHA: You mean like a circus clown.

ASAGAI: Well, as a matter of fact . . .

(She reaches out and puts both her fingers in his eyes.)

Actually, you delight me for a lot of reasons — including being a clown.

BENEATHA (Mockingly): Oh, ha, ha, ha!

ASAGAI: You're so eager for compliments. What do they do to the children in this country that one must constantly compliment people in order to have a conversation?

BENEATHA: I wasn't looking for a compliment, merely an answer.

ASAGAI: You're very much like some of our young people at home.

BENEATHA: You mean the ten-year-olds, of course?

ASAGAI: Now don't ask for insults.

CLOSE-UP—BENEATHA

BENEATHA: Are you a revolutionary?

ASAGAI: Yes, of course.

BENEATHA: Why "of course"?

ASAGAI: Because I suppose all Africans are rev-
olutionaries today, even those who don't know
that they are. It is the times. In order to survive
we must be against most of what is.

BENEATHA: I wish I were an African!

TWO SHOT

ASAGAI (*smiling*): So you could be a revolutionary?

BENEATHA: Yes, and a nationalist. I see all the
demonstrations in the newsreels. And I get a pain
right here (*touching her heart*). Millions of Africans marching, singing, carrying their leaders on
their shoulders. . . .

ASAGAI (*smiling even more*): You've seen only
thousands at most so far; and the shoulders of
other men is not a very good place for leaders.

BENEATHA (*picking up her books*): Why are you
always like that?

ASAGAI: Like what?

BENEATHA (*annoyed*): Always so . . .

ASAGAI: What?

BENEATHA: Well, so disparaging about all the
big things.

ASAGAI: You are serious enough about them for both of us, I think.

BENEATHA *(exhaling in anger as she arises)*: That's exactly what I mean.

ASAGAI: I don't know, perhaps it's because you're a woman and I can take women only just so seriously.

BENEATHA: *(very angry)*: Are you really so proud about being so backward about women?

ASAGAI: Am I backward about it?

BENEATHA: Pu-lenty.

ASAGAI: May I visit you tomorrow?

BENEATHA *(haughtily)*: I don't know—you'll have to call and see.

CLOSE-UP—ASAGAI *as he watches her walk away. Delight and admiration in his face.*

ASAGAI: That I will most certainly do.

DISSOLVE TO:

EXT.—FORTY-SEVENTH STREET—SHOPPING CENTER—SOUTH SIDE—DAY

The general bustle of a busy street.

EXT.—GROCERY AND MEAT MARKET

The store is a medium-size neighborhood affair of the variety that paints the day's specials right onto its windows:

"Fryers, spec. today: 29¢ lb." At least half of its inventory of vegetables and fruits are displayed out front of the store in open cartons.

MED. CLOSE SHOT—CLERK, LENA YOUNGER

A youngish CLERK, *white, stands in a white apron with his back turned to* LENA, *weighing a bulging bag. He notes the weight, tucks the top edges in, and turns with the bag to the counter. He is a bland and indifferent human being, inclined to treat his customers as though they trouble him by coming in.*

CLERK: Okay—what else?

QUICK FLASH—LENA'S FACE BEFORE CAMERA RETURNS TO MED. SHOT

Simmering annoyance with him rises in her face, and she keeps her hands folded in front of her in irritation as her eyes scan the closed bag and the CLERK's *face.*

LENA: H'you get them apples in that bag so fast?

MED. CLOSE SHOT—TO INCLUDE CLERK

CLERK: Well, I ain't got all day to fool around here, moms.

CLOSE-UP—LENA

LENA: I look like your mother to you, boy?

MED. SHOT—TO INCLUDE CLERK

There is silence as the CLERK *ostentatiously rolls his eyes to the ceiling to actively signify* his *exasperation at the remark.*

LENA: Dump them apples out there so I can see 'em.

CLERK: Look, lady—

LENA: That's just what I aims to do. This is my money I'm spendin'.

She reaches out quickly and grabs the bag bottom-side and turns the apples out onto the counter. They are a dismal crew, and LENA's *face reflects the fact.*

Who was chewin' on 'em before you decided to sell 'em to me?

CLERK: You can always do your shoppping someplace else.

CLOSE SHOT—LENA'S FACE, OUTRAGED BY HIS IMPUDENCE

LENA: Was you brought up to talk to older people like that, or you just turned wild here late?

(She snaps her purse closed.)

MED. SHOT

CLERK: La-dy—

LENA: I'll have to do my shopping someplace else, all right. Till you all learn yourselves some manners in this place!

CLERK: For Christ's sake, suit yourself!

LENA *(turning away, fussing)*: Got the nerve to be askin' people thirty-five cents for them apples

look like they was on the scene when Moses
crossed over! Just think the Southside is the garbage dump of this city where you can sell all the
trash don't nobody else in America want. Wouldn't
be tryin' to sell 'em over yonder where I work. . . .

She turns to look into the smiling face of MRS. JOHNSON,
*a slightly built little lady who is her contemporary in years
and a neighbor.*

Oh—hello there, Johnson.

MRS. JOHNSON: Hello there yourself. Lord,
Lena, you still out here trying to change the
world.

LENA: I ain't trying to change nothing. I'm tryin'
to buy me some apples to make my family a
decent pie and these here bandits wants *thirty-
five cents* for some fruit that was at the Last Supper! And they gonna have to learn how to talk
to people. Come callin' me—

MRS. JOHNSON: You ain't never gonna learn
how to bend with the wind, are you, Lena? What
you doin' home so early? Half day?

LENA: Half day and *last* day. I'm through wor-
kin' today, Johnson.

CLOSE SHOT—MRS. JOHNSON

*There is wonder in her face at the news, then pleasure—then
inevitable envy.*

MRS. JOHNSON: Go on—you don't mean it!

TWO SHOT

LENA: 'Deed I do. Gonna sit down and look around heaven, Johnson.

MRS. JOHNSON: Praise God!

LENA: Praise God!

MRS. JOHNSON: Ain't that lovely. On account of the insurance money?

LENA: That's right!

MRS. JOHNSON: Lord, sometimes He works in mysterious ways . . . but He works, don't He?

LENA: He does, child, He does!

MRS. JOHNSON (*because she is inclined to rather gross insincerity, she puts out all good wishes rather excessively, with gestures to match*): Mmmmmmm! I know Brother 'n'em must be just so happy for you!

LENA (*radiant with pride*): You know they are. I was blessed with good children.

MRS. JOHNSON: I'll say. Well, I got to be getting on home. You comin'?

LENA: No, no, not this morning. I got me a notion to get on that streetcar and go on out where you can shop decent. . . .

CAMERA COMES DOWN on her happy face

DISSOLVE TO:

EXTREME CLOSE SHOT—LARGE, RED,
VOLUPTUOUS APPLES—DAY

Camera inspects the lush perfection of the fruit and moves
back to:

WIDER ANGLE TO INCLUDE STALLS OF OTHER
HANDSOME FRUITS AND VEGETABLES

LENA, *in foreground, is contentedly paying* CLERK, *also
white, for several bags of fruit.*

CAMERA MOVES BACK FOR:

EXT.—HIGH WIDE-ANGLED SHOT—DAY—
MARKET

To show that she is in the famous "open markets" of the
far South Side, where the world's finest produce is exhibited for blocks and blocks in the open air. This is a specific
scenic Chicago landmark.

LENA *completes her transaction and turns to leave.*

DISSOLVE TO:

INT.—CROWDED MOVING STREETCAR
(PROCESS)—DAY

LENA *rides along on inside seat near window, her parcels
on her lap. She looks around the car and out the window
at random. One chance glance notices area where the houses
have turned into comfortable one- and two-family affairs.*

MED. LONG SHOT—HOUSE—P.O.V.: LENA
FROM STREETCAR WINDOW

A young white woman, wrapped for the chill, is dragging a small boy into the house from the sidewalk and a cluster of toys and playmates. The house is small, neat, attractive, and too much like every single other one on the block. There is a tiny lawn with a few brand-new trees stuck in the ground—and all viewers are certain it is the kind that has a small, fenced-in backyard.

CLOSE-UP—LENA'S FACE

She twists her head mightily to keep the house in view as long as possible, an expression of unabashed longing filling her eyes.

DISSOLVE TO:

INT.—CROWDED MOVING BUS (PROCESS)—DAY

WALTER, *in his own clothes, hangs from a strap, pressed on all sides by people coming home from work. He looks out of the window with random interest in the people and the neighborhood, which is his own. At one corner he sees:*

LONG SHOT—EXT.—HERMAN'S LIQUORS

Neighborhood liquor store, reasonably prosperous-looking with well-stocked windows and a blinking neon assertion.

QUICK FLASH—WALTER'S FACE

It shows moment of indecision about something, which passes, and he stays on bus resolutely.

EXT.—BUS PULLING TO STOP AT WALTER'S CORNER

He gets off, squeezing himself between those who are trying to get off and on.

MED. CLOSE TRACKING SHOT

Camera goes with him down his street. It is late afternoon.

Children play street games, and WALTER *knows one or two of them. He speaks to them or cuffs them playfully with extreme absent-mindedness as he approaches his stoop.*

MED. STATIONARY SHOT AT STOOP

He puts one foot on the stoop and stops.

CLOSE SHOT—WALTER'S FACE

He reconsiders something, makes a decision, and turns.

LONG SHOT—THE STREET

WALTER *is half-running back toward the liquor store.*

EXT.—LIQUOR STORE—MEDIUM SHOT

WALTER *comes onto the scene with brisk step, slows, halts, turns, and walks away. He goes a few steps, decides, and turns and enters store.*

INT.—LIQUOR STORE—GENERAL SCENE

A Negro CLERK *in a crisp, gray clerk's jacket turns from the shelves to wait on him.*

> CLERK: Hi, Walt. What can I give you?

> WALTER: Nothing today, Sammie. I want to talk to Herman.

> CLERK: I'll call him. How's the family?

WALTER (*preoccupied*): Uh—fine, man, fine. Thanks. How's yours?

CLERK: Growin'. Edna's expectin'. Hey, Herman!

CLOSE SHOT—BACK WORKROOM—HERMAN— LIQUOR STOCK IN BACKGROUND

HERMAN, a balding, middle-aged white man in vest and rolled shirtsleeves, is opening a liquor carton and stops when his name is called.

HERMAN: Yeah—what is it, Sammie?

SAMMIE (*offscreen*): Walter Younger wants to see you up front.

HERMAN *sighs a little at being interrupted and puts down his tool.*

GENERAL SCENE—STORE

HERMAN *comes out and smiles in friendly fashion at* WALTER. *His manner and the mood of the scene establish the irony of noncommunication between two men. There is nothing "racist" in* HERMAN's *attitude to* WALTER LEE. *He is genuine, helpful, is simply voicing a typcial shopkeeper's plaint. It is* WALTER *who cannot understand.*

HERMAN: What's up, Walter my boy?

WALTER: Hello, Herman. Wondered if I could speak to you a little.

HERMAN: Sure.

He stands and waits. WALTER *flashes his eyes once toward Sammie, who understands.* WALTER *and* HERMAN *move to a corner of the store.* WALTER *leans across the counter a little to talk.*

TWO SHOT—WALTER, HERMAN

> WALTER: I wanted to ask you a few questions about something if you got the time.

> HERMAN: Go.

> WALTER: Well . . . I been kind of thinkin' 'bout goin' into business with some buddies of mine, you know?

> HERMAN: Oh? Never thought of you as a businessman, Walter. Always thought you had too much sense for this kind of headache, boy!

He suddenly guffaws and slaps WALTER *on the arm.* WALTER *misses the joke but is not offended. He smiles lamely and goes on.*

> WALTER: I mean we sort of had a place just about like this in mind—you know what I mean? You do all right, don't you, Herman? I mean, I don't mean to be getting in your business or nothin' . . .

CLOSE FLASH—HERMAN'S FACE

His laughter fades as he realizes the man is deeply serious.

> HERMAN: Well, now, just a minute, Walter. You serious?

TWO SHOT

WALTER: Yes, I might be gettin' my hands on a little money soon—thought maybe you could give me a little advice.

HERMAN *(scandalized, in manner):* And you're thinking about doing something like this! *(Shaking his head with a sense of doom:)* Oh, Walter, am I glad you came in to talk to me first! *(He puts one hand on* WALTER'*s shoulder and leans close to him across the counter with a great air of confidence.)* If you only knew the headaches—if you only knew the headaches! Listen, son, I'm talking to you like a real father now. Don't do it. If you only knew what I would give to have a nice nine-to-five job again like what you got. . . .

CLOSE-UP—WALTER

The sudden beginnings of understanding flood his face, and with them, anger.

WALTER *(warmly)*: Then why don't you sell this and get yourself a nine-to-five, then?

TWO SHOT

HERMAN *(missing one-half the implications of the question because he is so certain* WALTER *could not mean exactly what he does)*: Listen, if you knew my wife you wouldn't even ask. I can promise you that. She's got a vocabulary of one word: "Gimme." Look, take it from me, fella, it ain't worth it. Keep what you got: a nice, simple life with some other sucker taking the headaches and the after-hour problems. I always say that the nine-to-five guys just don't know how good they got it.

CLOSE SHOT—WALTER

His eyes begin to get narrower and narrower as HERMAN *talks.*

CLOSE SHOT—HERMAN *who, somehow, believes every word of it at the moment.*

> HERMAN: Now you take this place. Fella like you walk in here and you look around and you think: "Say, that Herman, he's doing all right, boy!" *(He laughs.)* Well, let me tell you it ain't that pretty when you get inside the pot. You think I get to enjoy a nickel? *(Shaking his head at the thought of it:)* I could tell you stories about my overhead alone. . . .

TWO SHOT

> WALTER *(in open anger now)*: Man, what kind of overhead you got with bare floors and one man workin'!
>
> HERMAN *(shocked)*: Watsamatterwithyou, ain't you heard about the hours you have to put in when you're in business for yourself? You ask any retailer—why, I'm almost tempted to bring my books out and show you some things, my boy.

CLOSE SHOT—WALTER

> WALTER: You'll never be *that* tempted.

CLOSE SHOT—HERMAN

> HERMAN: What's the matter with you?

CLOSE SHOT—WALTER

WALTER: I'm thinkin' how big it is of you to want to keep me out of misery.

GENERAL SCENE—WALTER, HERMAN, SAMMIE

SAMMIE *is standing polishing a wine display and has heard the last of the conversation as it rose in volume. He watches with sympathy as* WALTER *suddenly turns on his heel and slams out of the door.*

MED. CLOSE SHOT OF HERMAN BEHIND COUNTER, ANGLED TO INCLUDE SAMMIE IN BACKGROUND

HERMAN: Now what do you make of that? To give people advice today is to take your life in your hands!

In his corner, SAMMIE *is motionless for a mere second then goes on polishing the bottles.*

DISSOLVE TO:

INT.—YOUNGER APARTMENT—EVENING— GENERAL SCENE

RUTH *is ironing from a large pile of rough dried clothes. For company she has on a gospel program, and the voice of Mahalia Jackson floods the room singing "Move On Up a Little Higher."* LENA *enters from the outside, carrying her packages.*

LENA: Hey there, Ruth.

RUTH (*genuinely glad to see her home*): Hi!

She puts down her iron and goes to help with the packages.

> LENA: Get on out the way, child—I can manage.
> *(She suddenly notices Ruth and puts down every-
> thing in her hands abruptly and takes hold of her
> daughter-in-law with both hands and looks at her
> very carefully.)* What's the matter with you?

RUTH *pulls away and tries to get out of immediate view by
getting back to the ironing board.*

> RUTH: Tired, I guess. Been ironing since this
> morning.

> LENA *(moving about, putting away the groceries,
> momentarily placated by the answer)*: Well, leave
> some of 'em for me. I'll get to 'em tonight.

RUTH *wheels sharply at the ironing board and faces her.*

> RUTH: You think that what we want you home
> for is so that you can start doin' everybody else's
> work now?

> LENA *(touched by the concern)*: Aw, little ironing
> ain't never hurt nobody. And the way you look
> you need to sit down most 'mediately. Bet you
> got a touch of that virus goin' 'round. Don't look
> no better than you do tomorrow you better stay
> home.

> RUTH: I have to go in. She's doin' her Saturday-
> night entertainin'. She have a fit if I don't show
> up.

LENA *has put away her things and inspected everything in
the apartment with some detail and settles heavily into a
chair to remove her street shoes and put on her slippers.*

LENA: Well, just let her have it. I call up first thing in the morning and tell her you got the flu.

RUTH *(half-laughing)*: Why the flu?

LENA: You know. It always sounds so respectable to white people. They know about the flu. Otherwise they think you been cut up or something when you tell 'em you sick. *(Looking about suddenly:)* Where's my baby at this hour?

RUTH: Ain't come in yet.

LENA: He got on his coat?

RUTH *(suddenly realizing that her business is being meddled with)*: No, just his lumber jacket.

LENA: Awful cold for a child to be running round with just a jacket on.

RUTH *(poised for battle on the issue, one hand on her hip)*: Lena . . .

LENA: I ain't meddlin'. I just noticed that you hadn't started giving him hot cereals yet in the morning, and when it starts gettin' this cold a child have to be fed warmer and dressed warmer—

RUTH *(real anger)*: I look after my son, Lena!

LENA: I ain't meddlin'! *(Pause.)* What did you give him this mornin'?

RUTH *(with fury)*: Hot oats, is that all right?!

LENA: I ain't meddlin'. *(Pause.)* Put a lot of nice butter on it? *(Pause.)* He likes lots of butter.

She gathers up her street shoes and carries them to a closet and sticks them in it. She then goes to the window and peers out of it a bit.

I wonder what's keepin' Miss Beneatha so late today. It's almost five.

EXT.—CLOSE SHOT—A SMALL AND GRUBBY LITTLE PLANT IN POT ON SILL

LENA *looks at it through the window and lifts window and brings it in.*

MED. CLOSE SHOT—LENA, PLANT

She touches its leaves with pained tenderness.

LENA: Lord, if this little plant don't start gettin' more sunlight than it's been gettin' it ain't never gonna see spring again.

She pushes in the dirt around the stem with her fingers, sets it back on the sill and closes the window.

FULL SHOT—GENERAL SCENE

RUTH *goes on with her ironing;* LENA *starts to put on an apron.*

LENA *(feeling her back)*: Hmmm. Little tired— had to go all the way yonder out to the markets to get decent groceries.

RUTH *(putting down her iron in exasperation at the remark)*: Ain't you never going to learn to go do your shoppin' in the supermarkets, Lena? What you think they built 'em for? Goin' way out there!

LENA: I can't stand all them buggies rollin' around and belts movin' and my meat lookin' all wrapped up like candy. Them places frighten me. *(Noting Ruth again:)* Honey, you sure lookin' like you could fall over right there. I know you ain't goin' out of here to do nobody's work tomorrow.

RUTH: I got to go. We need the money.

LENA: Child, we got a great big old check comin' tomorrow.

RUTH: Now, that's your money. It ain't got nothin' to do with me. We all feel like that. Walter and Bennie and me. Even Travis.

CLOSE SHOT—LENA SITTING DOWN TO DRINK COFFEE

LENA: Ten thousand dollars.

RUTH: Sure is wonderful.

LENA: Ten thousand dollars.

WIDER ANGLE TO INCLUDE RUTH IRONING

RUTH *(animatedly, sincerely as she works)*: You know what you should do, Miss Lena? You should take yourself a trip somewhere—to South America or Europe someplace. Just pack up and go off and finally have yourself a ball in this life.

LENA: Now, Ruth, what would I look like wanderin' round Europe by myself?

RUTH: Shoot—these here rich white women do it all the time. They don't think nothing of packing up they suitcases and—*swoosh!*—they gone, child!

LENA: Something always told me I wasn't no rich white woman.

CLOSE SHOT—RUTH AT BOARD

Her face reveals the duality of her feelings: her strong feelings that LENA *will use the money only for her own joys mingled right beside a hope that she might use it otherwise.*

RUTH: Well, what are you goin' to do with it, then?

CLOSE SHOT—LENA

LENA: I ain't rightly decided, to tell the truth. *(Reflectively:)* Of course, a good part of it got to be put away for Beneatha's medical schoolin' and all. That goes without sayin'. Ain't nothin' goin' to touch that part of it. *Nothin'.*

She waits several seconds, trying to make up her mind about something, and looks up at RUTH *a little tentatively before going on.*

Was sort of thinking—just think, mind you—that maybe—that we could maybe meet the notes on a little old two-story someplace, if we use part of the insurance money for a down payment and everybody kind of pitch in. . . .

CLOSE SHOT—RUTH

She lifts her head slowly as the thought penetrates, and her eyes rove around the beaten apartment almost involuntarily, taking in its decrepit state.

RUTH: Well, the Lord knows we put enough rent into this here rat trap to pay for four houses by now.

FULL SHOT—TO INCLUDE APARTMENT

LENA (*looking around and sighing*): "Rat trap"— yes, that's about all it's gettin' to be. But I remember just as well the day me and Big Walter moved in here. Hadn't been married but two weeks and wasn't planning on livin' here no more than a year. We was goin' to set away little by little and buy a little place out in Morgan Park. Had even picked out the house.

CLOSE SHOT—LENA

(*laughing a little to herself*) Looks right dumpy today. But you should know all the dreams I had about buyin' that house and fixin' it up; makin' me a little garden out in back. . . . And didn't none of it never happen. . . .

She looks to the couch as:

PANNING SHOT FOLLOWS HER EYES TO COUCH

(*offscreen*): Honey, Big Walter would come in here some nights back then and slump down on that couch there and just look at the rug. He'd sit there and just stare at that rug and then back at me. I'd know he was down then. Really down. And when we lost that baby . . .

CLOSE SHOT—LENA

. . . I almost thought I was going to lose Big Walter, too. Oh, that man grieved hisself. He was one man to love his children. . . .

MED. CLOSE SHOT—RUTH

RUTH: Yes, guess ain't nothin' can tear at you like losin' your baby.

CLOSE SHOT—LENA

LENA: I guess that's how come that man finally worked hisself to death like he done. Like he was fightin' his own war with this here world that took his baby from him. Sure loved his children. Used to say: "Seem like God didn't see fit to give the black man nothin' but dreams—but he did give us children to make them dreams seem worthwhile." *(She smiles.)* He could talk like that, don't you know.

GENERAL SCENE—FULL SHOT

RUTH: Yes, he sure could! He was a good man, Mr. Younger.

BENEATHA, *dressed in raincoat and kerchief, enters in a hurry, with books. She puts down the books and starts to rush around, getting ready to go back out.*

LENA: Well, did you decide to come home? I thought your last Friday class was over at three-thirty?

BENEATHA: It is, but I started my guitar lessons today.

She rushes into her bedroom for something. RUTH *puts down her iron to look at* LENA, *who meets her eyes with the identical sense of the confounded.*

LENA *(to the room)*: You started your *what* kind of lessons?

BENEATHA *(offscreen)*: GUITAR!

RUTH *and* LENA, *already poised for laughter since the initial remark, now roar.*

RUTH: Oh, Father!

LENA *(to the room)*: How come you done taken it in your head to learn to play the guitar?

BENEATHA *comes out of the bedroom, buttoning up a date dress.*

BENEATHA: I just want to, that's all.

LENA *(laughing softly)*: Lord, child, don't you know what to do with yourself? How long it goin' to be before you get tired of this now like you got tired of that little play-actin' group you joined last year? *(Looking at* RUTH.*)* And what was it the year before that?

RUTH: The horseback riding club for which she bought that fifty-five-dollar ridin' habit that's been hanging in the closet ever since!

LENA: Why you got to flit so from one thing to another, baby?

BENEATHA: I just want to learn to play the guitar. Is there anything wrong with that?

LENA: Ain't nobody tryin' to stop you. Just wonders sometimes why you has to flit so from one thing to another all the time. You ain't never done nothin' with all that camera equipment you brought home—

BENEATHA: I don't "flit"—I experiment with different forms of expression.

RUTH: Like riding a horse?

BENEATHA (*sharply, to* RUTH): People have to express themselves in one way or another.

LENA (*innocently, baffled*): Well, what is it you want to express?

BENEATHA (*with anger*): ME!

RUTH *and* LENA *look at each other again and burst into a roar of raucous laughter.*

Don't worry—I don't expect you to understand, for chrissakes!

LENA: Bennie!

RUTH: Just listen to her—just listen!

BENEATHA: Oh, God!

LENA: If you use the Lord's name just one more time . . .

BENEATHA (*a bit of a whine*): Oh, Mama!

RUTH: Fresh—just fresh as salt, this girl!

BENEATHA *(saucily)*: Well—if the salt loses its savor . . .

LENA: Now that will do. I just ain't going to have you round here reciting the Scriptures in vain—you hear me?

BENEATHA: How did I manage to get on everybody's wrong side just by walking into a room?

LENA *(suddenly noticing that* BENEATHA *is getting rather dressed up)*: Where you goin'?

BENEATHA: Got a date. *(Sighing:)* George Murchison again.

LENA: Oh, gettin' a little sweet on him?

RUTH: You ask me, this child ain't sweet on nobody but herself. *(Under her breath:)* Express herself!

BENEATHA: God no! George is all right to go out with and stuff, but—

RUTH: What does "and stuff" mean?

LENA: Stop pickin' at her now, Ruth. *(Double take.)* What *does* it mean?

BENEATHA *(wearily)*: Oh, I just mean I couldn't ever really be serious about George. He's so—shallow.

RUTH: What you mean he's "shallow"? He's *rich*!

BENEATHA *(sighing even more heavily)*: Oh, Ruth, anybody who married Walter could not possibly understand what I am talking about.

LENA *(scandalized)*: What kind of way is that to talk about your brother?

BENEATHA *(dryly)*: Brother is a flip—let's face it!

LENA *(helplessly, to* RUTH*)*: What's a flip?

RUTH: She's sayin' he's crazy.

LENA *turns to defend her son with vigor, but* BENEATHA *waves the protest down.*

BENEATHA: Not crazy. Brother isn't really crazy yet. He—he's an elaborate neurotic.

LENA: Hush your mouth now!

BENEATHA: As for the Murchisons . . . Well, George's mother wouldn't want me to marry George any more than I would ever want to marry George!

LENA: And why not?

BENEATHA: Because the Murchisons are honest-to-God real live rich colored people, and the only people in the world who are more snobbish than rich white people are rich colored people. Thought everybody knew that by now.

LENA *(innocently, unprepared for the class war)*: You must not dislike people 'cause they well off, honey.

RUTH: Don't worry, Lena. She'll get over all of this. That's just youth talkin' now.

BENEATHA: Get over it? What are you talking about, Ruth? Listen, I am going to be a doctor. I am not even worried about who I am going to marry yet. If—I ever get married.

RUTH and LENA (*involuntary unison*): *If!*

LENA: Now, Bennie—

BENEATHA: Oh, I probably will—but first I am going to be a doctor, and George, for one, still thinks that is pretty funny. I couldn't be bothered with that. I am going to be a doctor and everyone around here better understand that!

LENA (*pleasantly*): 'Course you goin' to be a doctor, honey, God willin'.

BENEATHA: God hasn't got a thing to do with it.

CLOSE SHOT—LENA

LENA: Beneatha—that last just wasn't necessary.

CLOSE SHOT—BENEATHA

BENEATHA: Well, neither is God. I get sick of hearing about God all the time.

TWO SHOT—LENA, BENEATHA

LENA: Beneatha!

BENEATHA: I mean it. I'm just tired of hearing about God all the time. What has he got to do with anything? Does he pay tuition?

LENA: You're 'bout to get your fresh little jaw slapped.

RUTH: That's what she needs, all right. Fresh as salt—

BENEATHA *(to her mother)*: I don't see why I can't say what I want around here like everybody else!

LENA: 'Cause it don't sound nice for a young girl to say things like that. You wasn't brought up that way. Me and your daddy went to trouble to get you and Brother to church every single Sunday!

CLOSE SHOT—BENEATHA

BENEATHA: Mama, you don't understand. It's all a matter of ideas, and God is just one idea I don't accept. It's not important. I am not going out and commit crimes or be immoral because I don't believe in God. I don't even think about it. It's just that I get so tired of Him getting credit for all the things the human race achieves through its own stubborn effort. There simply is no God! There is only Man, and it's he who makes miracles!

FULL SHOT—LENA, BENEATHA, RUTH

RUTH *halts the ironing altogether, sensing a crisis.* LENA *absorbs her daughter's speech and rises from her chair and crosses to her daughter and slaps her powerfully across the face. There is silence then as the mother stands before the daughter, her hands folded in front of her.*

LENA: Now—you say after me: "In my mother's house there is still God." *(Silence.)* "In my mother's house there is still God."

BENEATHA *(finally intimidated)*: In my mother's house there is still God.

The older woman turns and walks away from the girl.

MED. CLOSE SHOT—LENA—LOW-ANGLED

LENA: There's some ideas we ain't goin' to have in this house. Not long as I am head of this family. . . .

She turns and goes offscreen into her room.

CLOSE SHOT

BENEATHA: *(defeated)*: Yes, ma'am.

FULL SHOT—RUTH, BENEATHA

BENEATHA *puts on her coat.* RUTH *looks at her with sympathy.*

RUTH: You got treated like a little girl 'cause you was blurting out things like a little girl.

BENEATHA *(at door)*: I see. I also see that everyone thinks it's all right for Mama to be a tyrant.

She opens the door and slams out. RUTH *goes to her mother-in-law's door and pushes it open a little.*

RUTH *(to make a dishonest peace)*: She said she was sorry.

LENA *comes out of the room and wanders a little.*

LENA *(turning on Ruth)*: They frightens me, Ruth, my children.

RUTH: You got good children—they just a little off sometimes.

LENA *wanders to the kitchen window and opens it.* RUTH *starts her ironing again.*

MED. CLOSE—PLANT IN WINDOW, LENA

LENA: No—there's something come down between me and them that don't let us understand each other, and I don't know what it is. One almost done lost his mind thinking about money all the time and the other done commence to talk about things I can't understand in no form or fashion. What is it that's changing, Ruth?

RUTH *(offscreen)*: Now . . . you taking it all too seriously. You just got strong-willed children, and it takes a strong woman like you to keep 'em in hand.

LENA *(looking at her plant and shaking a little water on it)*: They spirited all right, my children. Got to admit they got spirit—Bennie and Walter. Like this little old plant that ain't never had enough sunshine or nothing—and look at it. . . . *(She closes the window gently.)*

CLOSE SHOT—RUTH

with her own thoughts.

> RUTH: Lena—what are you goin' to do 'bout helpin' him?

TWO SHOT

LENA *turns slowly to look at her daughter-in-law,*
understanding.

> LENA: You mean Walter? 'Bout his liquor store and all? What old Willy Harris want him to invest in?

> RUTH: Yes. *(She drops her head.)* I'm worried for him, Lena.

LENA *watches her carefully.*

> I mean I'm worried for what can happen to him if something don't happen for him soon. Something important to him. Something that makes him feel like he can beat this world.

> LENA *(looking away from her and frowning with distaste)*: But liquor, honey . . .

> RUTH: Well, like Walter Lee say, I 'spec people always goin' to be drinkin' themselves some liquor.

> LENA: Yes, but that don't mean I'm the one got to be sellin' it to 'em. It's gettin' too close to the time for me to meet my Maker to be havin' that on my ledger. 'Sides, we ain't no business people, Ruth. We just plain workin' folks.

> RUTH: Walter Lee say ain't nobody business people till they go into business. He says colored

people ain't goin' to never start gettin' ahead until they start gamblin' on some different kinds of things in this life. Investments and things.

LENA: What's done got into you, girl? Walter Lee done finally sold you on investin'?

RUTH: No. Mama, something is happening between Walter and me. I don't know what it is— but he needs something—something I can't give him anymore. He needs this chance, Lena.

LENA (*she turns back toward window*): Well, ain't no use of it. I ain't puttin' the memory of my husband into no liquor. (*She is looking out of the window.*)

WIDER-ANGLED SHOT INCLUDES RUTH, *who has stopped ironing once more and placed both hands on the board to steady herself; she makes a valiant effort to remain standing and talking lest* LENA *notice her true condition.*

(facing out window) Lord, ain't nothin' as dreary as the view from this window on a dreary day, is there?

Behind her, RUTH *slips silently and quietly to the floor.*

Why ain't you singin' none today, girl? Sing that old "No Ways Tired"—song always cheers me up so. . . .

She turns to see her daughter-in-law lying quite unconscious under the ironing board.

DISSOLVE TO:

EXT.—A NEIGHBORHOOD LOUNGE—THE
GREEN HAT—NIGHT

A typical neighborhood show-lounge. It is not a honky-
tonk. Neon is inescapable, but the place is otherwise
attractive.

INT.—A SIDE BOOTH—FOREGROUND:
WALTER, BOBO, WILLY HARRIS—WIDE
ANGLE TO INCLUDE

some background of the bar, where the usual clusters of
people sit or stand. Among them is a reasonable cross-
section of the community. Yet no one comes here in over-
alls or uniforms of labor. There are, in fact, one or two
young men standing about who are noticeably dapper. It
is a place to which the men would bring their wives, and
the atmosphere should suggest that. The custom of coming
to such a place when one is dressed properly is rooted in
the tradition of people who have never been welcomed in
the truly "swank" clubs and night spots of the Loop and
who have therefore invested "their" places of this type on
the Southside with as much importance as they can. To go
here is to "go out." To the camera it will seem, then, an
ordinary-looking dark American show-lounge; to them, it
is one of the "better places," which, in fact, has its main
reward in the fact that the people who patronize it and
several others like it on the Southside have unwittingly had
the historical experience of hearing before the rest of the
world most of the developments in jazz, of all schools, as
it came north. Such a sound invades the place now. A
saxophone is going in deep and indescribable alto perfection behind the dialogue. It is played by a great musician
as likely as a mediocre one. The patrons know it, and tend
to listen more carefully and appreciatively than future audiences at other places the man will someday play. He is
backed up by a drum, a bass, and piano; all play with soul.
(E.g.: "Mood Indigo" à la Johnny Hodges.)

MED. CLOSE SHOT—WALTER, BOBO,
WILLY HARRIS

As the music goes under WALTER *turns to face* BOBO *and* WILLY. *There are beer bottles and glasses on the table in front of them.* WILLY *is speaking emphatically.*

> WILLY: Yeah, man, that's the way the grays are. They figure if you join 'em, you beat 'em. Last thing they want to see is a Negro going into business.

> WALTER: You should of seen that clown just standin' there lookin' at me, talkin' about "my boy, you don't know the headaches."

He makes the "shh" sound with his lips. The other two men laugh knowingly. WILLY HARRIS *is an emphatic, persuasive fellow.* BOBO *is a quiet, slightly defeated man. Both are in their late forties.*

> WILLY: I tell you, if we could ever swing this thing, man, I got connections of some people who are interested in settin' up a chain.

> WALTER: A chain?

> WILLY: Sure—I can't be interested in no two-by-four operation no more, man. One of these days, I expect to see my stores in every city worth talkin' about. 'Cause that's one thing you can believe, people gonna be drinkin' themselves some booze when like they can't even be makin' it with the rent, right?

> BOBO: That's a fact. That's strictly a fact.

WILLY (*to* WALTER): So if you would just get up off some bread, man, we got this thing made.

CLOSE SHOT

WALTER *is looking off to the stars then shakes his head as the real situation of his life intrudes.*

WALTER (*smiling gently; softly at first*): Yeah, but man, you don't know the situation at home. Three women at the barricades, you know what I mean? And if there is somebody who cannot be persuaded to take a larger view in this world, it is a woman!

MED. SHOT TO INCLUDE WILLY, BOBO

They laugh with acclaim for what they consider the recognizable truth of the remark.

WILLY: That's right, they're something! I mean, they are a mistake!

BOBO: That's right—like every time I've been next to a scheme, I mean close, something really shakin', my wife say (*mimicking*), "Bobo, you ain't gonna be takin' my money and foolin' around with none of that stuff."

WILLY (as they laugh again): That's why it's time to break out. What you say, Walter?

CLOSE-UP—WALTER

WALTER (*lifting his glass*): I say it's a deal!

MED. CLOSE

The other two look at him, smile, and lift their glasses.

FADE OUT

FADE IN:

INT.—YOUNGER APARTMENT—MORNING

It is Saturday morning. BENEATHA is spraying insecticide about the apartment while her mother is washing down the kitchen wall. TRAVIS stands about restlessly, wanting to go out and play but lacking permission to do so.

FULL SHOT—GENERAL SCENE

TRAVIS: Grandmom, that stuff Bennie's usin' smells awful. Can I go downstairs, please?

LENA: You got all your chores done? I ain't seein' you doin' much.

TRAVIS: Where did Mama go, since she didn't go to work this morning?

LENA *(looking at* BENEATHA*)*: She had to go on a little errand.

TRAVIS: Where?

LENA: To tend to her business. *(With harassed spirit:)* And for pity's sake go on out and play. But stay right in front of the house. *(As he flies out:)* And keep a sharp lookout for the postman.

TRAVIS *(poking his aunt as he passes her)*: Leave them ole cockroaches alone, they ain't botherin' you none.

He runs as she swings the spray gun at him, both viciously and playfully. He exits.

LENA: Look out there, girl, before you be spillin' some of that stuff on that child.

BENEATHA: I can't imagine that it would hurt him—it has never hurt roaches. Mama, where did Ruth go?

LENA: To the doctor, I think.

BENEATHA: The doctor? What for? *(Silence.)* You don't think—

LENA: I ain't sayin' what I think. But I ain't never been wrong about a woman neither.

The telephone rings. BENEATHA *goes to answer.*

BENEATHA: Hay-lo. . . . Oh. . . . I don't think you can, Asagai. . . . We've got housecleaning and all that, and my mother hates it if I let people come over when the house is like this. . . . Oh, you have? . . . Oh, what the hell, come on over. . . . Right. See you then! *(She hangs up.)*

LENA *(who has listened vigorously, as is her habit)*: Who is that you inviting over here with this house looking like this? You ain't got the pride you was born with!

BENEATHA: Asagai doesn't care how houses look, Mama—he's an intellectual.

LENA: Who?

BENEATHA: Asagai—Joseph Asagai. He's an African boy I met on campus.

LENA: What's his name?

BENEATHA: Asagai, Joseph. Ah-sah-guy . . . He's from Nigeria.

LENA: Oh, that's the little country that was founded by slaves way back. . . .

BENEATHA: No, Mama—that's Liberia.

LENA: I don't think I never met no African before.

BENEATHA: Well, do me a favor and don't ask him a whole lot of ignorant questions about Africans. I mean, do they wear clothes and all that. . . .

LENA: Well, now, I guess if you think we so ignorant round here maybe you shouldn't bring your friends here.

BENEATHA: It's just that people ask such crazy things. All anyone seems to know about when it comes to Africa is Tarzan.

LENA (indignantly): Why should I know anything about Africa?

BENEATHA: Why do you give money at church for the missionary work?

LENA: Well, that's to help save people.

BENEATHA: You mean save them from heathenism.

LENA (*innocently*): Yes.

BENEATHA: I'm afraid they need more salvation from the British and the French.

RUTH *comes in forlornly and pulls off her coat with dejection. They both turn and look at her.*

RUTH (*dispiritedly*): Well, I guess from all the happy faces—everybody knows.

BENEATHA: You pregnant?

CLOSE SHOT—LENA

LENA: Lord have mercy, I sure hope it's a little ole girl. Travis ought to have a sister.

WIDER ANGLE TO INCLUDE BENEATHA AND RUTH *who give her a hopeless look for this grandmotherly enthusiasm.*

BENEATHA: How far along are you?

RUTH: Two months.

BENEATHA: Did you mean to? I mean, did you plan it or was it an accident?

LENA: What do you know about planning or not planning!

BENEATHA: Oh, Mama.

RUTH (*wearily*): She's twenty years old, Lena.

BENEATHA: Did you plan it, Ruth?

RUTH: Mind your own business.

BENEATHA: It is my business—where is he going to live, on the roof?

There is silence following the remark as the three women react to the sense of it.

Gee—I didn't mean that, Ruth, honest. Gee, I don't feel like that at all. I—I think it is wonderful.

RUTH *(dully)*: Wonderful.

BENEATHA: Yes—really.

LENA *(looking at Ruth, worried)*: Doctor say everything going to be all right?

RUTH *(far away)*: Yes—she says everything is going to be fine. . . .

LENA *(immediately suspicious)*: "She"? What doctor you went to?

RUTH *folds over, near hysteria.* LENA *worriedly hovers over her.*

Ruth, honey—what's the matter with you—you sick?

RUTH *has her fists clenched on her thighs and is fighting hard to suppress a scream that seems to be rising in her.*

BENEATHA: What's the matter with her, Mama?

LENA (*working her fingers in* RUTH's *shoulder to relax her*): She be all right. Women gets right depressed sometimes when they get her way. (*Speaking softly, expertly, rapidly:*) Now you just relax. That's right . . . just lean back, don't think 'bout nothing at all . . . nothing at all . . .

RUTH: I'm all right. . . .

The glassy-eyed look melts, and then she collapses into a fit of heavy sobbing. The bell rings.

BENEATHA: Oh, my God—that must be Asagai.

LENA (*to* RUTH): Come on now, honey. You need to lie down and rest a while . . . then have some nice hot food.

They exit, RUTH's *weight on her mother-in-law.* BE-NEATHA, *herself profoundly disturbed, opens the door to a smiling* JOSEPH ASAGAI, *who is rather dramatically carrying a large package.*

MED. CLOSE ASAGAI—LOW-ANGLED

ASAGAI: Hello, Alaiyo.

FULL SHOT—GENERAL SCENE

BENEATHA (*holding the door open and regarding him with pleasure*): Hello. . . . (*Long pause.*) Well—come in. And please excuse everything. My mother was very upset about my letting anyone come here with the place like this.

ASAGAI (*coming into the room*): You look disturbed, too. . . . Is something wrong?

BENEATHA *(still at the door, absently)*: Yes . . . we've all got acute ghetto-itus. *(She smiles and comes toward him, finding a cigarette and sitting.)* So—sit down! *(She presses her hands together, in a deliberately childish gesture.)* What did you bring me?

ASAGAI *(handing her the package)*: Open it and see.

BENEATHA *(eagerly opening the package and drawing out some records and the colorful robes of a Nigerian woman)*: Oh, Asagai! . . . You got them for me! . . . How beautiful! . . . And the records, too! *(She lifts out the robes and runs to the mirror with them and holds the drapery up in front of herself.)*

ASAGAI *(coming to her at the mirror)*: I shall have to teach you how to drape it properly. *(He flings the material about her for the moment and stands back to look at her.)* Ah—Oh-pay-gay-day, oh-gbah-mu-shay *(a Yoruba exclamation for admiration)!* You wear it well. . . . *(He stands back from her and folds his arms across his chest as he watches her at the mirror.)* Do you remember the first time you met me at school? *(He laughs.)* You came up to me and you said—and I thought you were the most serious little thing I had ever seen—you said *(he imitates her)*, "Mr. Asagai— I want very much to talk with you. About Africa. You see, Mr. Asagai, I am looking for my identity!" *(He laughs.)*

CLOSE—BENEATHA

BENEATHA *(turning to him, not laughing)*: Yes. . . ? *(Her face is quizzical, profoundly disturbed.)*

MED.—ASAGAI

ASAGAI (*still teasing, and reaching out and taking her face in his hands and turning her profile to him.*): Well . . . it is true that this is not so much a profile of a Hollywood queen as perhaps a queen of the Nile. . . . (*A mock dismissal of the importance of the question:*) But what does it matter? Assimilationism is so popular in your country.

CLOSE—BENEATHA

BENEATHA (*wheeling; passionately, sharply*): I am not an assimilationist!

MED. CLOSE—ASAGAI

He allows her protest to hang a moment in the room as he studies her, his laughter fading.

ASAGAI: Such a serious one. (*Pause.*) So—you like the robes? You must take excellent care of them—they are from my sister's personal wardrobe.

TWO SHOT—BENEATHA, ASAGAI

BENEATHA: You—you sent all the way home— for me?

ASAGAI (*charmingly*): For you—I would do much more. . . . Well, that is what I came for. I must go.

BENEATHA: Will you call me, Monday?

ASAGAI: Yes, we have a great deal to talk about. I mean, about identity and time and all that.

BENEATHA: Time?

ASAGAI: Yes—about how much time one needs to know what one feels.

FULL SHOT

She moves back from him suddenly with characteristic exasperation.

BENEATHA: You have never understood, apparently, that there is more than one kind of feeling which can exist between a man and a woman— or at least, there *should* be more than one kind of feeling!

ASAGAI *(laughing a little at her again)*: No. Between a man and a woman there need be only one kind of feeling. And I have that for you. Now even—right this moment—

BENEATHA: I know! And by itself it won't do. I can find that anywhere. . . .

ASAGAI *(smiling)*: For a woman it should be enough.

BENEATHA *(with spirit)*: I know—because that's what it says in all the novels that *men* write.

He roars.

But it isn't. Go ahead and laugh—but I'm not interested in being someone's little episode in America—or one of them!

He laughs even louder.

That's funny as the dickens, huh?!

ASAGAI: It's just that every American girl I have known has said that to me. White—black—in this you are all the same. And the same speech, too.

BENEATHA *(angrily)*: Yuk, yuk, yuk!

ASAGAI: It's how you can be sure that the world's most liberated women are not liberated at all. You all talk about it too much!

LENA *enters from* RUTH's *bedroom and is immediately and instinctively all social grace and charm because of the presence of a guest. The two younger people are also a little still because of her presence.*

BENEATHA: Mama—Mama, this is Mr. Asagai.

CLOSE SHOT—LENA'S FACE, GLOWING

LENA: How do you do.

MED. CLOSE—GROUP

ASAGAI: How do you do, Mrs. Younger. Please forgive me for coming at such an outrageous hour on a Saturday.

LENA *(sustaining her determination to demonstrate her respectablility to her daughter)*: Well, you are quite welcome. I just hope you understand that our house don't always look like this. *(A quick look to her daughter, then, chatterish:)* You must come again. I would love to hear all about—*(uncertain)*—your country. I think it's so sad the way our American Negroes don't seem to know nothin' 'bout Africa 'cept Tarzan and all that. And the money they pour into these churches when they ought to be helping you people over there drive out them French and Englishmen done taken away your land.

Upon the completion of the newly learned recitation, the mother flashes a slightly superior look at her daughter. ASAGAI *and* BENEATHA *are astonished.*

ASAGAI: Well, yes—yes, thank you.

LENA *(relaxing in the face of her accomplishment and looking him over as she might any woman's son a long ways from home)*: How many miles is it from here to where you come from, son?

ASAGAI: Many thousand.

LENA: And I bet you don't half look after yourself neither, being away from your mama and all. 'Spec you better come round from time to time and get yourself some decent home-cooked meals.

ASAGAI *(touched)*: Thank you. Thank you very much.

All are quiet and gratified by how well the meeting has gone. Then:

Well, I must be off. I will call you Monday, Alaiyo.

LENA: What's that he calls you?

ASAGAI: Oh— "Alaiyo." I hope you don't mind. It is what you would call a nickname. It is a Yoruba word. I am a Yoruba.

LENA *(thoroughly confused)*: I thought you said he was from—

ASAGAI: Oh, Nigeria is my country. Yoruba is my tribal origin.

BENEATHA: You didn't tell us what "Alaiyo" means. . . . For all I know, you might be calling me "Little Idiot" or something. . . .

ASAGAI: Well . . . let me see . . . I do not know how just to explain it. . . . The sense of a thing can be so different when it changes languages.

BENEATHA: You're evading.

TWO SHOT—ASAGAI, BENEATHA

ASAGAI: No—really it is difficult. . . . *(Thinking:)* It means . . . it means "One for Whom Bread—Food—Is Not Enough." *(He looks at her.)* Is that all right?

BENEATHA *(understanding, softly)*: Thank you.

WIDER ANGLE TO INCLUDE LENA *looking from one to the other and not understanding any of it.*

LENA: Well . . . that's nice. . . . You must come see us again—Mr.—

ASAGAI: Ah-sah-guy.

LENA: Yes . . . Do come again.

ASAGAI: Goodbye.

He exits.

LENA *(after him)*: Lord, that's a pretty thing just
went out here! *(Insinuatingly, to her daughter:)*
Yes, I guess I see why we done commence to get
so interested in Africa round here. Missionaries,
my Aunt Jenny!

She exits.

FULL SHOT—BENEATHA

BENEATHA *picks up the Nigerian dress and holds it up to
herself in front of the mirror again. She sets the headdress
on haphazardly and then notices her hair and clutches at it
and then replaces the headdress and frowns at herself. Then
she starts to wriggle in front of the mirror as she thinks a
Nigerian woman might. Travis enters and regards her.*

CAMERA WIDENS TO GENERAL SCENE

TRAVIS: You cracking up?

BENEATHA: Shut up.

*She pulls the headdress off and looks at herself in the mirror
and clutches at her hair again and squinches her eyes as if
trying to imagine something. Then, suddenly, she gets her
raincoat and kerchief and hurriedly prepares for going out.*

LENA *(coming back into the room)*: She's resting
now. Travis, baby, run next door and ask Mrs.

Johnson to please let me have a little kitchen cleanser. This here can is empty as Jacob's kettle.

TRAVIS: I just came in.

LENA: Do as you told.

He exits. Lena looks at her daughter.

Where you going?

BENEATHA *(halting at the door)*: To become a queen of the Nile!

She exits in a breathless blaze of glory.

RUTH *appears in the bedroom door.*

LENA: Who told you to get up?

RUTII: Ain't nothing wrong with me to be lying in no bed for. Where did Bennie go?

LENA *(drumming her fingers)*: Far as I could make out—to Egypt.

RUTH *just looks at her.*

What time is it getting to?

RUTH: Ten-twenty. And the mailman going to ring that bell this morning just like he done every morning for the last umpteen years.

TRAVIS *comes in with the cleanser can.*

TRAVIS: She say to tell you that she don't have much.

LENA (*angrily*): Lord, some people I could name sure is tight-fisted! (*Directing her grandson:*) Mark two cans of cleanser down on the list there. If she that hard up for kitchen cleanser, I sure don't want to forget to get her none!

RUTH: Lena—maybe the woman is just short on cleanser.

LENA (*not listening*): Much baking powder as she done borrowed from me all these years, she could of done gone into the baking business!

The bell sounds suddenly and sharply, and all three are stunned—serious and silent. In spite of all the other conversations and distractions of the morning, this is what they have been waiting for—even TRAVIS, *who looks helplessly from his mother to his grandmother.* RUTH *is the first to come to life again.*

RUTH (*to Travis*): Get down them steps, boy!

TRAVIS *snaps to life and flies out to get the mail.*

CLOSE SHOT—LENA

LENA (*her eyes wide, her hand to her breast*): You mean it done really come?

CLOSE SHOT—RUTH

RUTH (*excited*): Oh, Miss Lena!

CLOSE SHOT—LENA

LENA (*collecting herself*): Well . . . I don't know what we all so excited about round here for. We known it was coming for months.

RUTH: That's a whole lot different from having it come and being able to hold it in your hands . . . a piece of paper worth ten thousand dollars. . . .

LONG SHOT—HIGH ANGLE

TRAVIS *bursts back into the room. He holds the envelope high about his head, like a little dancer; his face is radiant, and he is breathless. He moves to his grandmother with sudden slow ceremony and puts the envelope in her hands.*

CLOSE SHOT—LENA SLOWLY SINKS INTO A CORNER OF THE SOFA. CAMERA WIDENS TO GENERAL SCENE, RUTH STANDING BEHIND HER, TRAVIS AT HER KNEE

She accepts it, and then merely holds it and looks at it.

RUTH: Come on! Open it. . . Lord have mercy, I wish Walter Lee was here!

TRAVIS: Open it, Grandmama!

LENA *(staring at it)*: Now you all be quiet. It's just a check.

RUTH: Open it. . . .

LENA *(still staring at it)*: Now don't act silly. . . . We ain't never been no people to act silly 'bout no money—

RUTH *(swiftly)*: We ain't never had none before—open it!

Mama finally makes a good strong tear and pulls out the thin blue slice of paper and inspects it closely. The boy and his mother study it raptly over Mama's shoulders.

LENA: Travis! *(She is counting off with doubt.)* Is that the right number of zeros?

CLOSE SHOT—TRAVIS

TRAVIS: Yes'm . . . ten thousand dollars. Gaallee, Grandmama, you rich.

CLOSE SHOT—LENA

She holds the check away from herself, still looking at it. Slowly her face sobers into a mask of unhappiness.

LENA: Ten thousand dollars. *(She hands it to* RUTH.*)* Put it away somewhere, Ruth. *(She does not look at* RUTH: *her eyes seem to be seeing something somewhere very far off.)* Ten thousand dollars they give you. Ten—thousand—dollars!

GROUP SHOT

TRAVIS *(to his mother, sincerely)*: What's the matter with Grandmama—don't she want to be rich?

RUTH *(distractedly)*: You go on out and play now, baby.

TRAVIS *exits.* LENA *starts wiping dishes absently, humming intently to herself.* RUTH *turns to her with kind exasperation.*

You've gone and got yourself upset.

TWO SHOT

LENA *(not looking at her)*: I 'spec if it wasn't for you all . . . I would just put that money away or give it to the church or something.

RUTH: Now, what kind of talk is that? Mr. Younger would just be plain mad if he could hear you talking foolish like that.

LENA *(stopping and staring off)*: Yes . . . he sure would. *(Sighing:)* We got enough to do with that money, all right.

She halts then and turns and looks at her daughter-in-law hard. RUTH *avoids her eyes.* LENA *wipes her hands with finality and starts to speak firmly to* RUTH.

Where did you go today, girl?

CLOSE—RUTH

RUTH *(evasively)*: I went to the doctor.

MED.

LENA *(impatiently)*: Now, Ruth . . . you know better than that. Old Dr. Jones is strange enough in his way, but there ain't nothing 'bout him make somebody slip and call him "she," like you done this morning.

CLOSE

RUTH: Well, that's what happened—my tongue slipped.

MED.

LENA: You went to see that woman, didn't you?

CLOSE

RUTH *(defensively, giving herself away)*: What woman you talking about?

FULL SHOT

LENA *(angrily)*: That woman who—

WALTER *enters in great excitement.*

WALTER: Did it come?

LENA *(quietly)*: What you doing home at this hour? And can't you give people a Christian greeting before you start asking about money?

WALTER *(to Ruth)*: Did it come?

RUTH *unfolds the check and lays it quietly before him, watching him intently with thoughts of her own.* WALTER *sits down and grasps it close and counts off the zeros.*

Ten thousand dollars. *(He turns suddenly, frantically to his mother and draws some papers out of his breast pocket.)* Mama—look. Old Willy Harris put everything on paper. . . .

LENA: Son—I think you ought to talk to your wife. I'll go on out and leave you alone if you want.

WALTER: I can talk to her later. Mama, look—

LENA: Son—

CLOSE—WALTER

WALTER: WILL SOMEBODY PLEASE LISTEN TO ME—TODAY!

MED.

> LENA *(quietly)*: I don't 'low no yellin' in this
> house, Walter Lee, and you know it.

WALTER *stares at them in frustration and starts to speak*
several times.

> And there ain't going to be no investing in no
> liquor stores. I don't aim to have to speak on
> that again.

A long pause.

CLOSE

> WALTER: Oh—so you don't aim to have to speak
> on that again? So you have decided . . . *(crum-*
> *pling his papers:)* Well, you tell that to my boy
> tonight when you put him to sleep on the living-
> room couch. . . . *(Turning to* LENA *and speaking*
> *directly to her:)* Yeah—and tell it to my wife,
> Mama, tomorrow when she has to go out of here
> to look after somebody else's kids. And tell it to
> me, Mama, every time we need a new pair of
> curtains and I have to watch you go out and work
> in somebody's kitchen. Yeah, you tell me then!
> *(He starts out.)*

FULL SHOT—GENERAL SCENE

> RUTH: Where you going?

> WALTER: I'm going out!

> RUTH: Where?

WALTER: Just out of this house somewhere—

RUTH *(getting her coat)*: I'll come too.

WALTER: I don't want you to come!

RUTH: I got something to talk to you about, Walter.

WALTER: That's too bad.

LENA *(still quietly)*: Walter Lee. . . .

She waits, and he finally turns and looks at her.

Sit down.

WALTER: I'm a grown man, Mama.

LENA: Ain't nobody said you wasn't grown. But you still in my house and my presence. And as long as you are—you'll talk to your wife civil. Now sit down.

RUTH *(suddenly)*: Oh, let him go on out and drink himself to death! He makes me sick to my stomach! *(She flings her coat against him.)*

WALTER *(violently)*: And you turn mine too, baby!

RUTH *goes into their bedroom and slams the door behind her.*

That was my greatest mistake.

LENA *(still quietly)*: Walter, what is the matter with you?

WALTER: Matter with me? Ain't nothing the matter with me!

LENA: Yes there is. Something eating you up like a crazy man. Something more than me not giving you this money. The past few years I been watching it happen to you. You get all nervous-acting and kind of wild in the eyes—

WALTER *jumps up impatiently at her words.*

I said sit there now, I'm talking to you!

WALTER: Mama—I don't need no nagging at me today.

LENA: Seem like you getting to a place where you always tied up in some kind of knot about something. But if anybody ask you 'bout it you just yell at 'em and bust out the house and go out and drink somewhere. Walter Lee, people can't live with that. Ruth's a good, patient girl in her way—but you getting to be too much. Boy, don't make the mistake of driving that girl away from you.

WALTER: Why—what she do for me?

LENA: She loves you.

WALTER: Mama—I'm going out. I want to go off somewhere and be by myself for a while.

LENA: I'm sorry 'bout your liquor store, Son. It just wasn't the thing for us to do. That's what I want to tell you about.

WALTER: I got to go out, Mama. *(He rises.)*

CLOSE—LENA

LENA: It's dangerous, son.

CLOSE—WALTER

WALTER: What's dangerous?

CLOSE—LENA

LENA: When a man goes outside his house to look for peace.

MED.—WALTER

WALTER *(beseechingly)*: Then why can't there never be no peace in this house, then?

CLOSE—LENA

LENA: You done found it in some other house?

CLOSE—WALTER

WALTER: *(angrily)* No—there ain't no woman! Why do women always think there's a woman somewhere when a man gets restless? *(Coming to her:)* Mama—Mama—I want so many things. . . .

FULL SHOT—WALTER, LENA

LENA: Yes, Son.

WALTER: I want so many things that they are driving me kind of crazy. . . . Mama—look at me.

LENA: I'm looking at you. You a good-looking boy. You got a job, a nice wife, a fine boy, and—

WALTER: A job. (*Looks at her.*) Mama, a job? I open and close car doors all day long. I drive a man around in his limousine and I say, "Yes, sir"; "No, sir"; "Very good, sir"; "Shall I take the Drive, sir?" Mama, that ain't no kind of job. . . . That ain't nothing at all. *(intently:)* Mama, I don't know if I can make you understand.

LENA: Understand what, baby?

WALTER *(quietly)*: Mama—sometimes when I'm downtown and I pass them cool, quiet-looking restaurants where them white boys are sitting back and talking 'bout things . . . sitting there turning deals worth millions of dollars . . . sometimes I see guys don't look much older than me. . . .

LENA: Son—how come you talk so much 'bout money?

WALTER *(with immense passion)*: Because it is life, Mama!

LENA *(quietly)*: Oh . . . *(Very quietly:)* So now it's life. Money is life. Once upon a time freedom used to be life—now it's money. I guess the world really do change. . . .

WALTER: No—it was always money, Mama. We just didn't know about it.

LENA: No . . . something has changed. *(She*

looks at him.) You something new, boy. In my
time we was worried about not being lynched and
getting to the North if we could and how to stay
alive and still have a pinch of dignity too. . . .
Now here come you and Beneatha—talking 'bout
things we ain't never even thought about hardly,
me and your daddy. You ain't satisfied or proud
of nothing we done. I mean that you had a home;
that we kept you out of trouble till you was
grown; that you don't have to ride to work on
the back of nobody's streetcar. You my children—but how different we done become.

WALTER: You just don't understand, Mama, you
just don't understand.

LENA: Son—do you know your wife is expecting
another baby?

WALTER *stands, stunned, and absorbs what his mother has
said.*

That's what she wanted to talk to you about.

WALTER *sinks down into a chair.*

CUT TO:

QUICK FLASH—RUTH IN HER BEDROOM—
MED. CLOSE SHOT

RUTH *moves across bedroom toward door. Halts and
listens.*

LENA'S VOICE *(offscreen)*: This ain't for me to
be telling—but you ought to know. *(Pause.)* I

think Ruth is thinking 'bout getting rid of that child.

WALTER'S VOICE *(offscreen; slowly understanding)*: No—no . . . Ruth wouldn't do that.

LENA'S VOICE *(offscreen)*: When the world gets ugly enough—a woman will do anything for her family. The part that's already living.

WALTER'S VOICE *(offscreen)*: You don't know Ruth, Mama, if you think she would do that.

FULL SHOT—LIVING ROOM

RUTH *opens the bedroom door and stands there, a little limp.*

RUTH *(beaten)*: Yes I would too, Walter. *(Pause.)* I gave her a five-dollar down payment.

There is total silence as the man stares at his wife and the mother stares at her son. Presently:

LENA: Well . . . ? *(Tightly:)* Well, son, I'm waiting to hear you say something. . . . I'm waiting to hear how you be your father's son. Be the man he was. . . . *(Pause.)* Your wife say she going to destroy your child. And I'm waiting to hear you talk like him and say we a people who give children life, not who destroys them. I'm waiting to see you stand up and look like your daddy and say we done give up one baby to poverty and that we ain't going to give up nary another one. . . . I'm waiting.

WALTER: Ruth . . .

LENA: If you are a son of mine, tell her!

WALTER *turns, looks at her, and can say nothing. She continues bitterly.*

You . . . you are a disgrace to your father's memory. Somebody get me my hat.

FADE OUT

FADE IN:

INT.—THE YOUNGER APARTMENT—NIGHT— RUTH

Camera moves back to show RUTH *faithfully at her ironing board ironing; in place of gospel music she is enjoying a rock-and-roll program.*

MED. SHOT—BENEATHA'S BEDROOM DOOR *which is thrust open with a loud bang as she emerges from it.*

CLOSE FALSE FLASH—RUTH, *who looks over her shoulder once to see why the noise and does an automatic double-take.*

FULL SHOT—BENEATHA *in the costume* ASAGAI *brought her; she promenades out and parades it before the astonished* RUTH. *She is grand in manner and deadly serious.*

GENERAL SCENE

RUTH: Well, what have we got on tonight?

BENEATHA: You are looking at what a well-dressed Nigerian woman wears. Isn't it beautiful?!

*Mid-sentence her senses are suddenly offended by the real-
ization of the nature of the music playing noisily in the
room. She advances to the radio and turns it off with a
flourish and turns to* RUTH:

Enough of this assimilationist junk!

MED. SHOT—BENEATHA—ANGLED TO INCLUDE
DUMBFOUNDED RUTH *in background, watching as her
sister-in-law puts a record on the phonograph and closes her
eyes and waits for the sound of music. A lovely Nigerian
melody comes up.* BENEATHA *keeps her eyes closed and
begins to move in rhythm to it. As it proceeds, her movement turns to an imaginative if desperately inauthentic
dance.*

RUTH: What kind of dance is that?

BENEATHA: A folk dance.

RUTH: What kinds of folks do that, honey?

BENEATHA: It's from Nigeria. It's a dance of
welcome.

*She dances with ambition about the apartment, not without
grace and rhythm in her intensity.*

RUTH: Who you welcoming?

BENEATHA: The men. Back to the village.

RUTH *(innocently)*: Where they been?

BENEATHA *(with exasperation)*: Oh, Ruth, how
should I know! Out hunting or something. Any-
way, they're coming back now.

RUTH: Well, that's good.

CLOSE SHOT—BENEATHA'S FACE

She starts to sing with the record, and the hauntingly quiet loveliness of the melody dominates the scene.

> BENEATHA *(poetically improvising)*:
> *Alundi, alundi*
> *Alundi alunya*
> *Jop pu a jeepua*

CAMERA MOVES BACK TO INCLUDE RUTH *watching with new appreciation as* BENEATHA *continues to sing and dance.*

> BENEATHA: *Ang gu sooooooo*
> *Ai yai yae* . . .

GENERAL SCENE

The doorbell rings. RUTH *answers and admits* GEORGE MURCHISON, *who regards* BENEATHA *with sophisticated astonishment as her song and dance continue uninterrupted.*

> BENEATHA: *Aye aye aye—alundi—*

> GEORGE: Look, honey, we're going *to* the theatre. We're not going to be *in* it.

CLOSE SHOT—BENEATHA

She is outraged by the remark.

> BENEATHA: I don't like that, George.

GENERAL SCENE—GEORGE, RUTH, BENEATHA

RUTH: You expect this boy to go out with you looking like that?

BENEATHA (*looking at George*): That's up to George. If he's ashamed of his heritage . . .

GEORGE: Oh, don't be so proud of yourself, Bennie—just because you look eccentric.

BENEATHA: How can something that's natural be eccentric?

GEORGE: That's what being eccentric means—being natural. Get dressed.

CLOSE SHOT—BENEATHA

BENEATHA: Don't worry, George, I wouldn't expect someone like you to have an appreciation for great and ancient cultures. I know that *your* only aim is to utterly submerge yourself in the dominant and, in this case, oppressive culture.

GROUP SHOT—GEORGE, BENEATHA, RUTH

GEORGE: Oh, dear, dear, dear! Here we go! A lecture on the African past! On our Great West African Heritage! In one second we will hear all about the great Ashanti empires; the great Songhay civilizations; and the great sculpture of Benin—and then some poetry in the Bantu—and the whole monologue will end with the word "heritage"! (*Nastily:*) Let's face it, baby—your heritage is nothing but a bunch of raggedy-assed spirituals and some grass huts!

BENEATHA: Grass huts! . . . See there . . . you would rather stand there in your splendid ignorance and know nothing of the people who were the first to smelt iron on the face of the earth—

RUTH *quietly and determinedly moves between them and begins to firmly push* BENEATHA *toward her bedroom.*

Why, the Ashanti were performing surgical operations when the British—

RUTH *gets her behind the door and closes it.*

BENEATHA'S VOICE *(offscreen; insistently)*: — were still tattooing themselves with blue dragons.

RUTH *(with discomfort at what she considers the embarrassing behavior of a member of the family)*: Have a seat, George.

They both sit. RUTH *folds her hands rather primly on her lap, determined to demonstrate the civilization of the family.*

Warm, ain't it? I mean for September. *(Pause.)* Just like they always say about Chicago weather: if it's too hot or cold for you, just wait a minute and it'll change. *(She smiles happily at this cliché of clichés.)* Everybody says it's got to do with them bombs and things they keep setting off. *(Pause.)* Would you like a nice cold beer?

GEORGE: No, thank you. I don't care for beer. *(He looks at his watch.)* I hope she hurries up.

RUTH: What time is the show?

GEORGE: It's an eight-thirty curtain. That's just Chicago, though. In New York standard curtain time is eight-forty. *(He is rather proud of this knowledge.)*

WALTER *enters. He has been drinking.*

WALTER: Where's Mama?

RUTH: She ain't come back yet. *(To George:)* You get to New York a lot?

GEORGE *(offhand)*: Few times a year.

RUTH: Oh—that's nice. I've never been to New York.

WALTER *(chip on shoulder)*: New York ain't got nothing Chicago ain't. Just a bunch of hustling people all squeezed up together—being "Eastern." *(He turns his face into a screw of displeasure.)*

GEORGE: Oh— you've been?

WALTER: *Plenty* of times.

RUTH *(shocked at the lie)*: Walter Lee Younger!

WALTER *(staring her down)*: Plenty! *(Pause.)* What we got to drink in this house? Why don't you offer this man some refreshment? *(To George:)* They don't know how to entertain people in this house, man.

GEORGE: Thank you—I don't really care for anything.

WALTER *leans against the refrigerator, drinking beer, regarding* GEORGE *from head to toe.*

WALTER: Hey.

GEORGE *does not realize he is being addressed.*

Hey!

GEORGE: What?

WALTER: How come all you college boys wear them faggoty-lookin' white shoes?

CLOSE SHOT—GEORGE *as he absorbs, reacts, and visibly represses reaction.*

GENERAL SCENE

RUTH: Walter Lee!

WALTER: Well, they look funny as hell. White shoes—cold as it is!

RUTH *(to* GEORGE*)*: You'll have to excuse him.

WALTER: *(bitter about many things)*: Oh no he don't! Excuse me for what? What you always "excusing" me for? I'll excuse myself when I need to be excused! *(Pause.)* They look awful. Bad as them black knee stockings Beneatha wear out of here all the time.

RUTH: It's the college *style*, Walter.

WALTER: Style nothing. She look like she got burned legs or something. *(He promptly ignores her and turns his attention on the now completely hostile* GEORGE.*)* Hear your dad is thinking about buying that big hotel on the Drive, man.

GEORGE *nods, unwilling to speak to him.* WALTER *gets a chair and drags it across the room to get closer.*

TWO SHOT—WALTER, GEORGE

I think that's a pretty shrewd move. *(Tapping his head in appreciation:)* Your old man is all right, man. I mean, for—you know what I mean. I mean he thinks Big—geez, I wish I could get to talk to him! For once get to talk to somebody on this whole Southside who could understand my kind of thinking. *(He waits and then suddenly scrutinizes* GEORGE *closely.)* Fact, I got some ideas that I would like to tell you about. You must have some of your old man's stuff in you. . . . We ought to sit down and talk sometimes, man. I bet you and me even—*(In his eagerness he reaches out to touch the younger man.)*

GEORGE *(brusquely)*: Yes, sometimes we'll have to do that, Walter.

He pulls away to mark his disinterest. WALTER *reads the action precisely).*

CLOSE SHOT—WALTER

The rejection cuts him deeply.

WALTER: Yeah, well, when you get the time, man. I mean, I know you are a busy little boy. I know ain't nothing as busy as you college boys. With your fraternity pins and your white shoes.

QUICK FLASH—RUTH

RUTH *(pained by this display)*: Oh, Walter Lee—

CLOSE SHOT—WALTER

WALTER *(with maximum bitterness)*: I see you all the time—with the books tucked under your arms, going to your "clahsses." And for what! What you learning over there? They're filling up your heads with the sociology and the psychology—but are they teachin' you how to be a man? How to take over and run this world? How to run a rubber plantation or a steel mill? Naw. Just to talk proper and read books and wear them faggoty-lookin' white shoes. . . .

TWO SHOT

GEORGE *sighs and takes out a cigarette and lights it.*

GEORGE: You're all whacked up with bitterness, man.

WALTER *(leaning close in his face, passionately)*: And you? Ain't you got no bitterness—'bout nothin'? Don't you see no stars gleamin' nowhere that you ain't been able to reach out and grab? You happy? You contented little . . . Bitter? Man, I am a volcano. Bitter? I am a giant—surrounded by ants! Ants who can't even understand what the giant is talking about.

GENERAL SCENE

RUTH *(passionately and suddenly)*: Oh, Walter—ain't you with nobody!

WALTER *(violently)*: No! 'Cause ain't nobody with me! Not even my own mother!

RUTH: Walter, that's a terrible thing to say!

BENEATHA *enters, dressed for the evening in a cocktail dress and earrings.*

GEORGE: Well—hey, you look great.

BENEATHA: Let's go, George. See you all later.

RUTH: Have a nice time.

GEORGE: Thanks. Good night. *(To* WALTER, *sarcastically:)* Good night, *Prometheus.*

BENEATHA *and* GEORGE *exit.*

CLOSE SHOT—WALTER

WALTER *(to* RUTH*)*: Who is Prometheus?

TWO SHOT

RUTH: I don't know. Don't worry about it.

WALTER *(in fury, pointing after* GEORGE*)*: See there—they get to a point where they can't insult you man to man—they got to go talk about something ain't nobody ever heard of!

RUTH: How you know it was an insult? *(To humor him:)* Maybe Prometheus is a nice fellow.

WALTER: Prometheus! I bet there ain't even no such thing! I bet that simple-minded clown—

GENERAL SCENE

LENA *enters and* WALTER *jumps up and shouts at her.*

Mama, where have you been?

LENA: My—them steps is longer than they used to be. Whew! *(She sits down and ignores him.)* How you feeling this evening, Ruth?

RUTH *shrugs and watches her husband knowingly.*

WALTER: Mama, where have you been all day?

LENA *(still ignoring him and leaning on the table and changing to more comfortable shoes)*: Where's Travis?

RUTH: Let him go out and he ain't come back yet again. Boy, is he goin' to get it.

WALTER: Mama!

TWO SHOT—WALTER, LENA—TO INCLUDE RUTH IN BACKGROUND

RUTH *watches them.*

LENA *(as if she has suddenly heard him)*: Yes, Son?

WALTER: Where did you go this afternoon?

LENA: Went downtown to tend to some business I had to take care of.

WALTER: What kind of business?

LENA: Now you know better than to question me like a child, Brother.

WALTER *brings his fists down on the table and shouts at her.*

WALTER: Mama, you didn't go out of here and do something with that insurance money—something crazy . . . ?

WIDER ANGLE—TO INCLUDE BACKGROUND, TRAVIS *who opens the door slowly and shows his head and carefully and quietly steps into the house, hoping not to be discovered.* RUTH *steps into the scene.*

TRAVIS: Mama, I—

RUTH: "Mama, I" nothing!

LENA: Why don't you all never let the child explain hisself?

RUTH: Keep out of it now, Lena. *(She advances toward the boy menacingly.)* A thousand times I have told you not to go off like that!

FULL SCENE—LIVING ROOM—RUTH, TRAVIS, LENA, WALTER

LENA *(holding out her arms to him)*: Well, let me tell him something I want him to be the first to hear. . . . Come here, Travis—come on, baby!

TRAVIS *slips rapidly to her, past his mother, as though she is a hot stove he is grateful to escape.* LENA *receives him in her arms.*

You know that money we got in the mail this morning?

TRAVIS: Yes'm.

LENA: Well, what you think your grandmama gone and done with that money?

TWO SHOT—TRAVIS, LENA

>TRAVIS: I don't know, Grandmama.

>LENA: She—she went out—and she bought you a house!

The exploding comes from offscreen: elsewhere in the room WALTER *has smashed glass or kicked the garbage can.* LENA *does not take her eyes off her grandson; she concentrates on the happiness that is possible in him and tries to ignore the pain of her son.*

>*(to* TRAVIS*)*: You glad about the house? It's gonna be yours when you get to be a man.

>TRAVIS: Yes'm. I always wanted to live in a house.

>LENA: All right. Give me some sugar then.

The boy puts his arms around her neck and kisses her.

>And when you say your prayers tonight, you thank God, and you thank your grandfather— 'cause it was him what give you the house—in his way.

RUTH *moves into the scene.*

>RUTH: Now you get on in there and get ready for your beating.

LONG SHOT—PAST WALTER'S FACE, VERY CLOSE, TO RUTH, LENA

WALTER's *jaws work with furious pulsing. Beyond,* RUTH *and* LENA *cast anxious glances at him.* RUTH *fairly pushes her son into her bedroom.*

TRAVIS: Aw, Mama—

RUTH: Get on in there!

She looks once with terror at her husband and then to her mother-in-law, but in spite of all her other feelings, radiance breaks onto her face and she comes rapidly to the older woman sitting at the table watching her son with hurt.

So—you went and did it!

LENA *(quietly)*: Yes I did.

RUTH *(raising both arms, classically, involuntarily, in exultation)*: Praise God!

She looks up at her husband, who remains where he is staring out of the window. She crosses to him.

Please, honey—let me be glad. You be glad too.

She puts her hands on his shoulders with supplication. He shakes them off, roughly, violently. He will not turn to her, and she begs him.

Walter . . . a *home*.

She turns and goes back to her mother-in-law, utterly caught in her own delirious emotion.

Well—where is it? How big is it? How much is it going to cost?

LENA: Well—

RUTH *(unable to wait)*: When we moving?

LENA *(smiling at her)*: The first of the month.

RUTH *(throwing back her head with the rapturous abandon of the delivered)*: PRAISE GOD!

WALTER's *bitter profile continues to edge the frame throughout the scene. His mother speaks to his attention, hopefully, while answering* RUTH.

LENA: It's—it's a nice house too. Three bedrooms. Nice big one for you and Ruth. Me and Beneatha will still have to share, but Travis'll have one of his own—and I figures *(to* RUTH*)* if the new baby is a boy, we could maybe get one of them double-decker outfits. . . . And there's a yard where I could maybe get to grow me a few flowers . . . and a nice big basement. *(nostalgically, without quite meaning to be:)* Your daddy was always so handy with his hands, he always wanted him someplace to set up a workroom.

RUTH: Honey—be glad!

LENA *(spiritedly)*: 'Course I don't want to make it sound fancier than it is. . . . It's just a plain little old house—but—it will be *ours*. Walter Lee, it makes a difference to a man when he can walk on floors that belong to *him*. . . .

RUTH *(innocently, her face lit)*: Where is it?

CLOSE SHOT—LENA

LENA: Well— *(a deep sigh)* well—it's out there in Clybourne Park.

LONG SHOT—AS BEFORE, INCLUDING WALTER'S PROFILE *as he turns, struck senseless at this last. In the background* RUTH *also halts and stares at her mother-in-law, who lifts her head a little, her jaw set.*

RUTH: Where?

LENA: 406 Clybourne Street, Clybourne Park.

RUTH *(with incredulity)*: Clybourne Park? There ain't no colored people living in Clybourne Park.

LENA *(a logician; meeting the absurdities of history with almost absurd logic)*: Well, I guess there's going to be some now.

WALTER *(a sudden shout)*: So that's the peace and comfort you went out and bought for us today!

LENA *(looking at him imploringly)*: Son, I just tried to find the nicest place for the least amount of money for the family.

GROUP SHOT

WALTER *advances on* LENA *and* RUTH *to absorb all the implications of the news.* RUTH *similarly casts her eyes back and forth from* LENA *to* WALTER, *trying to digest and resolve lest she lose something she has just gained in this life.*

RUTH: Well, of course I ain't never been one to be 'fraid of no crackers, mind you, but wasn't there no other houses nowhere?

LENA: Them houses they call theyselves putting up for colored way out yonder all seem to cost twice as much as other houses. I did the best I could.

LONG SHOT—HIGH ANGLE

RUTH, *herself struck senseless with the news, in its various degrees of goodness and trouble, sits a moment, her fists propping her chin in thought. But then overcome with the promise before her, she starts to rise, the radiance spreading from cheek to cheek once again.*

> RUTH: Well . . . well . . . all I can say is . . . if this is my time . . . my time to say goodbye— *(She begins to move about the apartment)* to these tired old cracking walls— *(she lets go and lets the walls have it with her fists, as the tears come)* — and these marching cockroaches! And this cramped little closet which ain't now and never was no kitchen! . . . Then I say it loud and good! Hallelujah! And goodbye, misery—I don't never want to see your ugly face again!

She has come to stand, in defiance, in the center of the apartment. LENA *watches this vision of a possibility that never happened for her when she was* RUTH's *age with her own restraint of a powerful emotion.* RUTH *stands, for the moment, indifferent to the nakedness of joy, with her chin tilted and her eyes seeing shimmering white walls somewhere.*

CLOSE SHOT—RUTH

Lena . . . ? Is there a whole lot of sunlight?

LENA: Yes, child, there is a whole lot of sunlight.

FULL SCENE—RUTH, LENA, WALTER

There is a long pause; presently, RUTH *collects herself and starts toward her bedroom.*

RUTH: Lord, I sure don't feel like whipping nobody tonight!

She goes out. The mother turns to the son.

LENA: Son—you understand what I done, don't you?

He stands near her in sullen silence.

I just seen my family falling apart today in front of my eyes. We couldn't of gone on like we was today. We was going backwards 'stead of forwards—talkin' 'bout killing babies and wishin' each other was dead. When it gets like that—you have to do something different; push on out and do something bigger. *(She waits.)* I wish you say something, son. Wish you say how deep inside you you think I done the right thing. . . .

WALTER *crosses suddenly toward his bedroom; he stops and turns abruptly to face her, pointing an accusing finger.*

WALTER: What you need me to say you done right for? You the head of this family! You run our lives the way you want to. It was your money and you did what you wanted to with it. So what you need me to say it was all right for? *(To hurt:)* So you butchered up a dream of mine—*you*—who always talking 'bout your children's dreams! . . .

LENA: Walter Lee!

He turns on his heels and closes the door with impact behind him. The mother sits on.

CLOSE SHOT—LENA'S NOW DEEPLY

TROUBLED FACE

FADE OUT

FADE IN:

INT.—BAR—WALTER DRINKING ALONE—
MED. CLOSE SHOT—NIGHT

Hold to establish mood of his drinking. (Cool-jazz themes
are introduced and stay through following montage.) Then:

DISSOLVE MONTAGE TO:

EXT.—CALUMET HIGHWAY—LONG SHOT—
NIGHT

A car roars along a ribbon of highway shooting south away
from the city; for miles on either side, flat marshlands border the highway, while at one side, edging Lake Calumet,
loom the steel mills of South Chicago, great black struc-
tures outlined against the glare of their own furnaces.

DISSOLVE MONTAGE TO:

INT.—CAR—CLOSE SHOT—WALTER—NIGHT

WALTER is driving intently, staring straight ahead.

EXT.—STATIONARY SHOT—THE MILLS—
ANGLED FROM BEYOND WALTER'S
PROFILE IN FOREGROUND—NIGHT

He simply stands staring at the industrial landscape, the
muscles of his jaws working in anguish.

EXT.—LONG SHOT—PANNING THE
STOCKYARDS—DAWN

Shot concludes by discovering WALTER leaning on a ramp above thousands of surging hogs or cattle, watching.

EXT.—LONG SHOT—SELECTED—MIDDAY

WALTER wandering aimlessly in the Loop; midday crowd about him.

INT.—BAR—WALTER DRINKING—NIGHT—
CLOSE-UP

His blues are now in total possession of him.

EXT.—THE SOUTHSIDE—DAWN—HIGH-
ANGLED SHOT

Shot discovers WALTER sitting on a curb in the early-morning shadow of the Negro Soldier's monument in a square at Thirty-Ninth and South Parkway; the streets are almost deserted, and he merely sits.

END OF DISSOLVE MONTAGE

FADE OUT

FADE IN:

EXT.—A STREET—SOUTHSIDE—MIDDAY—
LONG SHOT

WALTER comes upon a street meeting. He is still wandering in his dejection and indifferently finds a place in a crowd where an orator on a ladder is exhorting his listeners.

PANNING SHOT OF THE CROWD

It is made up in the main of men; inspection of their faces by camera shows that they listen with varying degrees of interest or agreement with the speaker who is skilled in his craft.

MED. SHOT—SPEAKER

He is a middle-aged man wearing a beard and a tired business suit and tie. He has one arm locked around a rung of the ladder, and the free arm pounds the air for emphasis. In immediate background we can see the American flag and a second, unfamiliar one designed with three simple horizontal colored bars, green, black, and red.

CLOSE SHOT—SPEAKER *turning his head to pick out the eyes of his listeners.*

> SPEAKER: And so, my black brothers, then what happens? Tell me, then what happens! The black man gets off the train day after day from Mississippi and Georgia—yes?

The crowd has not yet begun the almost automatic and rhythmical response which will eventually begin. They have heard many such speakers, and since what they talk about rarely changes, they linger mainly for the performance— waiting to see if this one or another can rouse them, if it will be a good performance. If it is, they will join him with shouts of approval and applause; if it is not, they will pass on and he will talk only to a few wanderers who have nothing else to do. This man is a good one, the rise and fall of his voice as dramatic as his commentary—not shrill or hysterical but resonant and compelling.

> And he gets here, and he looks around. *(Smiling bitterly, knowing that he is sharing a joke of indictment with his listeners:)* And he sees it: he is in Chicago—the Promised Land!

The crowd erupts with appreciative laughter.

LONG SHOT—HIGH WIDE-ANGLED—TO INCLUDE WALTER *who has wandered to the fringe area with his hands in his pockets.*

> SPEAKER *(with cutting sarcasm)*: The place where the streets are paved with gold and milk and honey flow from all fountains!

More laughter.

> And so the black man, he get off the train carryin' his one suitcase and he look around him and he think—Well, I'm here!

Roar of laughter.

PANNING SHOT—CLOSE—FACES IN THE CROWD

They are of many ages and classes now; the crowd has thickened, but few women, if any, have joined the group. The people have for the most part warmed to the speaker, because he is entertaining and colorful; some are already anxious for him to get on to the expected part of the harangue.

> *(offscreen)* And then what! He looks around and sees that the first thing he better do is get himself a job so he can take care of his babies and his wife. But that doesn't bother him, because isn't this the Promised Land?

Laughter.

> So he goes lookin' for a job. And who does he go to lookin' for this job? *(He waits.)* I am asking you. You know.

STATIONARY SHOT—SPEAKER—MED.

The crowd murmurs something a little uncomfortably, not yet ready to display itself.

He goes to the very man who has stolen his homeland, put him in bondage, defamed his nation, robbed him of his heritage! The White Man!

An involuntary shout of agreement roars up from the people, mingled with applause.

Get the spectacle of it if you dare: The White Man! And what does the white man do? Tell me, what does he do?

The crowd murmurs more vigorously than before. All laughter has died, and all eyes are riveted on the speaker as he exhorts them with undisguised passion.

Why don't you answer? We all know the answer! You go to him for a job and he hands you a broom!

A great shout of approval from the crowd. Angry and bitter "That's right!"'s arise.

LONG SHOT—CROWD, SPEAKER

Well, my brothers, it is time to ask ourselves what the black man is asking himself everywhere in this world today. . . .

Applause begins and dies.

Everywhere on the African continent today the black man is standing up and telling the white man that there is someplace for *him* to go—*(with a sudden burst of energy)*—back to that small, cold continent where he came from—Europe!

The camera pans away from him to the crowd again and fixes on

STATIONARY SHOT—ASAGAI'S FACE—MED. CLOSE

ASAGAI *stands impassively watching, as interested in the spectators as in the message of the speaker.*

SPEAKER *(offscreen):* Well, then—how long before this mood of black men everywhere else in the world touches us here? How long! How much has to happen before the black man in the United States is going to understand that God helps those who help themselves?

PANNING SHOT—SPEAKER, CROWD —P.O.V.: ASAGAI

His eyes scan the faces of the people around him. In the background, one among many, is the face of WALTER LEE, *listening.* ASAGAI *does not know him. Separated by many faces, they watch. The crowd cries out "True!" at the last of the speaker's remarks.*

I am here to tell you it's true! And what is the difference—what is the difference, my friends—between the black man here and every other man in the world? It's what every one of you knows—

PANNING SHOT—FACES OF CROWD

(offscreen) We are the only people in the world
who are completely disinherited!

A bitter cheer of agreement.

We are the only people in the world who *own*
nothing, who make nothing! I ask you, my
friends, where are your factories . . . ?

QUICK FLASH—WALTER'S FACE

CLOSE SHOT—SPEAKER

Heh? Where are your textile or steel mills?
Heh? Where are your mighty houses of finance? *(A pause as he looks intently at his listeners.)* ANSWER ME, MY BROTHERS—
WHERE ARE THEY?

MED. CLOSE SHOT—WALTER IN THE CROWD

*He closes his eyes to the words with a shudder and turns
away as the man goes on with his exhortation.*

WIDER ANGLE TO INCLUDE THE STREET—
EUROPEAN SPORTS CAR *which pulls up, containing*
GEORGE MURCHISON; *he calls out to* WALTER, *who recog-
nizes him and goes over.*

MED. CLOSE SHOT—CAR—WALTER, GEORGE

GEORGE: Hi, Walter. Where you going? Want a
lift?

WALTER *(looking back once to the meeting and
then shrugging)*: Yeah. You can drop me at the
Green Hat.

GEORGE: Geez. At this hour? Isn't it a little early, my friend? *(He regards* WALTER *with interest, suddenly noting his disheveled appearance and somewhat glazed-eye look.)*

WALTER: No, Dad, it's late. It is *very* late. *(He reaches out to take the handle of the car to open the door, but there is no outside handle.)* Say, man, what kind of toy is this you ridin' in?

GEORGE *opens the door from within and* WALTER *squeezes himself up with an excessive display of distaste to fit into the tiny car.*

INT.—MED. CLOSE—GEORGE, WALTER

WALTER *climbs in and looks around disparagingly.*

GEORGE: It's a *Twinkle*. British-made.

WALTER: Yeah, them people got problems. What's the matter, your old man gone broke?

GEORGE *(with some irritation)*: I bought the car because I like it, Walter. Maneuverability is the point. Get it? It is supposed to look like this.

WALTER: Yeah? Well, I'd rather maneuver me some power steering any day. Let's be off, my man.

They roar off as GEORGE's *energetic gear manipulations bang* WALTER's *knee.*

DISSOLVE TO:

EXT.—MEDIUM SHOT—DAY

The Twinkle pulls up in front of the Green Hat lounge.

INT.—CAR—TWO SHOT

GEORGE: You sure this is where you want to go,
Walter? Why don't you let me drive you home—
you look like you could use some sleep. . . .

WALTER (*glancing at him*): What's that? Loan a
man a deuce.

He holds out his hand without even looking at GEORGE.
GEORGE *sighs and looks at him and hauls out two bills and
gives them to him.*

EXT.—LONG SHOT—WALTER *who gets out of the car
and pushes the door closed with a flourish. He waves*
GEORGE *away and turns and goes into the bar.*

FADE OUT

FADE IN:

INT.—RUTH'S BEDROOM—NIGHT—MED. CLOSE

*She lies in the darkness on the bed, fully dressed. The tele-
phone rings from the living room off screen, and she jumps
up with a start to go answer it.*

MED. CLOSE SHOT—TELEPHONE SITTING ON
TABLE—RUTH *who comes onto scene and picks it up
with anxiousness.*

RUTH: Hello . . . Oh, Mrs. Arnold . . . Yes, this
is his wife . . . No—no, he isn't here just now.
(*A pause, then a quick and inventive, though uncertain, excuse:*) At the doctor's . . . Well, it was

the only appointment he could get. Yes, I know we should have called but we were so sure he would be able to come in today.

WIDER ANGLE TO INCLUDE DOOR WHERE LENA IS ENTERING SCENE

LENA *is immediately interested in the phone conversation. She stands and listens with deep disturbance on her face.*

RUTH: Yes . . . yes . . . of course. Well, I don't blame you. I'm very sorry. . . . Yes, yes—thank you. . . . Yes, all right. Thank you again.

She hangs up the phone, stands looking down at it.

LENA: What did they say?

RUTH *(starkly)*: They said they going to get somebody else if he don't come in tomorrow. Mr. Arnold been taking a cab for three days and she say she ain't going to have it. *(Suddenly, in a gasp, not for* MR. ARNOLD *and his cabs, of course, but for her husband:)* Oh, Lena, what's happening to him!

CLOSE SHOT—LENA

She looks at her daughter-in-law and then decides to do something. She puts her coat back on and takes up her hat and handbag in decisive gestures.

CLOSE SHOT—RUTH

Where you going?

MED. CLOSE—LENA, RUTH

LENA *(at the door)*: I'm going to get my boy. What's the name of that drinking place he goes to?

RUTH: Lena—it won't do any good. There ain't no point in your going after him. . . .

LENA *(sternly, not to be argued with)*: What's the name of it?

RUTH: The Green Hat.

LENA, *saying nothing, bundles her coat about her, opens the door and goes out with determination.*

DISSOLVE TO:

INT.—THE BAR—NIGHT—GENERAL SCENE

LENA *comes into the bar and stands resolutely, looking about for her son. One or two people look up and see her and are decidedly uncomfortable or are a little amused by her presence. She finally discovers* WALTER *at the end of the bar, sitting alone, drinking, listening to the music.*

LONG SHOT—WALTER AT BAR—P.O.V.: LENA

WALTER *sits on a stool, his eyes closed.*

CLOSE SHOT—ANGLED FROM WALTER IN FOREGROUND TO INCLUDE LENA ADVANCING TOWARD HIM IN BACKGROUND.

LENA *(in outrage)*: Get down from there this instant.

One or two people turn to note the scene. WALTER *turns his head slowly to see his mother. His face breaks into a smile of bitter amiability.*

WALTER: Why, hello there, Mama! *(He lifts his glass.)* Want a drink, Mama?

In a single gesture, without disturbing the hand that holds the pocketbook clasped in front of her, LENA *releases a blow which knocks the insulting glass from his hand; there is immediately stunned silence in the bar, except for her voice, which is controlled fury.*

LENA: You will get down off that stool, and you will walk out of this place this minute.

She stands and looks at him with both hands folded in front of her. There is total quiet in the bar.

CLOSE SHOT—WALTER'S FACE

He looks back at his mother through the mist of liquor which is controlling his senses. Suddenly, the flashing element of drunken defiance that first rose in his eyes dissolves and is replaced by total consciousness of who is confronting him. Momentarily closing his eyes, he slips down from the stool and walks past her to the door as the people watch. Lena motions to the bartender, who leans toward her, somewhat bewildered.

MED. CLOSE—LENA, BARTENDER

LENA *(perfunctory)*: Does he owe you money?

BARTENDER: Only for the last one. He had paid for everything else. That's eighty-five cents.

LENA *gives him a dollar.*

LENA: My change.

BARTENDER: Yes, ma'am.

He puts the money down. She counts it and picks it up and puts it in her purse and walks out.

DISSOLVE TO:

INT.—NEIGHBORHOOD LUNCHEONETTE—
MED. CLOSE SHOT—NIGHT

LENA *and* WALTER *sit in a booth together. Before him on the table are two cups and saucers. One cup is full and one empty. He has his hands in front of his face. His mother faces him with nothing in front of her, sitting very straight in her seat.*

> LENA: What have you been doing for the three days you ain't been to work, Walter Lee?
>
> WALTER: Mama . . .
>
> LENA: You aimin' to go the full circle now? How long before I have to come get you up from the sidewalks? You got hurt and pain in you? Well, I used to know a man who knew how to live with his pain and make his hurt work for him. Your daddy died with dignity; there wasn't no bum in him. And he known some hurts in this life you ain't never even heard of!
>
> WALTER (*suddenly lifting his head and looking at her*): Mama—why did you leave the South forty years ago?

His mother is halted by the question and merely sits looking at him, trying, perhaps, to discover if the question merely signifies that he is still drunk and incoherent.

CLOSE SHOT—WALTER *his face illuminated by the passionate question.*

I mean it, Mama. Tell me, why did you leave the South when you were a young woman?

CLOSE SHOT—LENA

LENA: I 'spect for the same reason everybody else does. I thought I might be able to do more with myself up here. And I don't say I exactly took over the world in the years since then, but—

TWO SHOT

WALTER: But you didn't give nobody the right to keep you there when you decided you had to go, did you, Mama? Even if you wasn't really goin' noplace at all—you felt like you was, didn't you, Mama, didn't you?!

CLOSE SHOT—LENA'S FACE

Set for a different argument, it slowly changes as she watches her son's face and absorbs his question and its implications. She sighs and leans back in her seat as though his particular truth of the moment is more than she can deal with. WALTER *leans forward to push it deeper.*

CLOSE SHOT—WALTER

(with enormous intensity; determined that she should understand if she has never understood before) Then why in the name of God couldn't you let me get on my train when my time came! *(Tightly—almost a whisper:)* I don't think it's going to come again, Mama. I don't think it's going to come again!

TWO SHOT

The mother and the son face each other. WALTER's *despera-tion has come home to the mother; she looks down at his hands, shaped, we might feel, somewhat like his father's; she closes her eyes—at once defeated and resurrected. With her eyes closed and exhaling with an exhaustion that is only now turning to a new determination, she opens her handbag and reaches into it.*

CLOSE SHOT—LENA

She places a roll of bills on table between them.

> LENA: I paid the man thirty-five hundred dollars down on the house. That leaves sixty-five hun-dred dollars. Tomorrow morning I want you to take this money and take three thousand dollars and put it in a savings account for Beneatha's medical schooling. The rest you put in a checking account—with your name on it. And from now on any penny that come out of it or that go in it is for you to look after. For you to decide. . . . It ain't much, but it's all I got in the world and I'm putting it in your hands. I'm telling you to be the head of this family from now on like you supposed to be.

> WALTER *(stares at the money)*: You trust me like that, Mama?

> LENA: I ain't never stop trusting you. Like I ain't never stop loving you.

Her son says nothing. He stares at the money, and then at his mother, who gathers her coat around her and gets up and goes out of the restaurant. WALTER *sits staring at the*

*money a long time before he finally reaches out his hand
and closes his fingers around the roll—as though he has
caught hold of the stars.*

FADE OUT

FADE IN:

CLOSE SHOT—WALTER'S HEAD *thrown back in the
most expressive, abandoned fit of laughter possible. The
laughter rises, builds, explodes, repeats itself—the laughter
of a thoroughly happy man.*

WIDER ANGLE SHOWS RUTH BESIDE HIM,
VERY CLOSE

They are dancing, and she too is lost in a fit of laughter.

> WALTER: We ought to name him Hezekiah after
> her mother's brother! That would fix Mama. She
> never could stand poor old Uncle Hezekiah!

They laugh again.

MED. CLOSE SHOT—RUTH, WALTER

They are dancing among other couples at a dance.

> RUTH: I wish I knew why everybody is so sure
> my baby just has to come here a boy. *(Looking
> up at him, happily:)* And I wish I knew some
> other things too. Like what's happened to my
> husband lately. . . .
>
> WALTER *(looking down at her with equal happi-
> ness)*: You'll find out when the time comes and
> not before.

He pulls her closer and they dance on.

CUT TO:

MED. SHOT—BENEATHA AND GEORGE

They are standing in an anteroom of the clubhouse, beyond the festivity of the dance. GEORGE leans close trying to kiss her; she feints, and he exhales with exasperation.

GEORGE: Look, we've had a nice evening. Let's not spoil it.

BENEATHA: I am trying to talk to you.

GEORGE: We always talk.

BENEATHA: Yes, I love to talk.

TWO SHOT

GEORGE: I know it. And I don't mind it, sometimes. But I want you to cut it out, see. All this moody stuff, I mean. I don't like it.

He starts to nuzzle her again.

BENEATHA *(reflective)*: George . . .

GEORGE: Yes?

BENEATHA: What are you going to do?

GEORGE: I am going to put my arms around you and—

BENEATHA: No, George, I'm serious.

CLOSE SHOT—GEORGE, BENEATHA

GEORGE *(exasperated)*: Okay. Okay. Finish school and go into business—what else? Get married. Simple. *(He advances again.)*

BENEATHA: George—I want to talk about us. To know us. I'd—I'd like to tell you some things about myself.

GEORGE: All right—so talk.

BENEATHA: It's—it's about—well, being a part of things.

GEORGE: What things?

BENEATHA: I mean, like—well—take my family.

GEORGE: Okay.

BENEATHA: Mama and Walter and Ruth and even Travis are all sort of rushing around trying to be like everybody else. Do you know what I mean? And do you know what *I* want, George—what I really want? All I want is the right to be *different* from everybody else—and yet—be a part too. . . .

GEORGE *(backing off hard)*: Oh—no. That's enough.

BENEATHA: Do you think everyone feels like that—down deep?

GEORGE: "Be different"—what the hell is with you? I mean, look—you're a nice-looking girl.

All over. That's all you need in this world, honey, so forget the atmosphere. They're going to go for what they see—be glad for that. Drop the Garbo routine. It doesn't go with you. *(Advancing again:)* As for myself—I want a nice—simple—sophisticated girl. I don't need a poet—okay?

She rebuffs him again, and he flares.

BENEATHA: Why are you angry?

GEORGE: Because this is stupid! I don't go out with you to discuss the nature of quiet desperation or something!

BENEATHA *(looking at him, studying him)*: I see. I—I'm glad we talked, George. I mean—I'm glad we tried—that *I* tried. It was very important. I mean, to try to tell you what I think about.

GEORGE: Why should it be important? The world will go on thinking what it thinks regardless—and I for one don't want everybody else's thoughts cluttering up my head.

BENEATHA: Then why read books? Why go to school?

GEORGE *(counting with artificial patience on his fingers)*: It's simple. You read books to learn facts—to get grades—to pass the course—to get a degree. That's all. It's got nothing to do with thoughts.

BENEATHA *(a long pause)*: I see. *(A longer pause as she looks at him.)* Thank you, George.

GEORGE: Yeah. You sleep on that tonight. *(Warming again:)* See if tomorrow you don't understand some of the things I've said.

BENEATHA: I understood them.

GEORGE *(suddenly subdued)*: Is everything all right?

BENEATHA: Yes—everything is fine now. Everything is fine.

BENEATHA *looks with absolute clarity at a now very chastened and confused* GEORGE, *as:*

GROUP SHOT

WALTER *and* RUTH *appear in the door and hail them.*

WALTER: Hey, Bennie—you know what Ruth just told me?

BENEATHA: What?

WALTER *(seeing* GEORGE; *condescendingly)*: Hey, man. You fraternity boys throw a nice function.

GEORGE *(smartly)*: Thanks, that's real big of you to say so.

WALTER *(the same)*: That's all right—anytime.

GEORGE: Do you approve of everything? How is the punch?

They are prepared to go on with this nonsense as RUTH *giggles.*

BENEATHA: What did Ruth tell you?

WALTER: Oh—do you know what your mother did?

BENEATHA: No.

WALTER: That woman went out and bought herself a house she has never even seen!

They laugh.

On account of the man what sold it to her told her she better not go out there and let them jokers see her till she was ready to move in!

They all laugh.

Yeah—she told Ruth. *(He waves them into a huddle of happy conspiracy.)* Lookahere—you know what we ought to do?

FADE OUT

FADE IN:

EXT.—TAXICAB PARKED AT CURB—LONG SHOT—DAY

RUTH, WALTER, BENEATHA, TRAVIS *sit in the cab anxiously watching the street in front of their apartment house. All are earnest in their manner but are visibly suppressing anticipatory giggles.* RUTH, *bursting most with delight, holds a large box; Beneatha a smaller one. It is* TRAVIS *who first sees their quarry.*

INT.—CAB—MED. CLOSE

TRAVIS: There she is now!

LONG SHOT—LENA WALKING ALONG SIDEWALK, CARRYING PACKAGES

CLOSE-UP—WALTER

WALTER: Wait till she gets a little closer. All right now, Son—advance!

LONG SHOT—HIGH ANGLES

They throw open the cab door, and WALTER *and* TRAVIS *leap out and race toward* LENA *like commandos. She is startled as they flank her and marshal her toward the cab. As she protests and questions them vigorously, they push her in the front seat and crowd themselves into the back as the two women conspicuously seek to conceal the unconcealable larger package.*

DISSOLVE TO:

EXT.—THE NEW HOUSE, A MODEST BUNGALOW—DAY—VERY BRIGHT SUNLIGHT

CAB PULLS UP ACROSS THE STREET

INT.—TWO SHOT—CABBIE, WALTER

CABBIE: That's 406, Mister.

He points to the house across the street. The faces of the family in the background turn in concert and look out at it. They are silent.

GROUP SHOT—CLOSE

It is to them a lovely house: rather more handsome than they had permitted themselves to dream; spanking new and clean, with a neat lawn out front and a quite precious fence. Each face regards it with its own reaction of disbelief. These are people who are primarily accustomed to disappointment; when things materialized in the past, they more often than not tended to be less than good, and very often were bad. RUTH *puts a finger or two to her lips;* BENEATHA *grins happily, mostly for her mother;* TRAVIS *merely grins; and* WALTER *himself first enjoys the sight of the house and them.*

CLOSE SHOT—LENA—P.O.V.: WALTER

He watches his mother's face, which is set with a joy that is almost painful to behold.

GROUP SHOT

Walter stirs first.

> WALTER: Well—get out! Everybody get out! Let's go in and have a look at it!

They bustle and stir out of the cab and collect absentmindedly in the street in front of the house, still staring at it.

LONG SHOT—HIGH-ANGLED—FAMILY
STANDING IN THE STREET LOOKING AT
THE HOUSE

TRACKING SHOT WITH THEM AS THEY
MOVE TOWARD AND INTO IT

INT.—LONG SHOTS—CUMULATIVE

They stand in silence and regard the place for several awed seconds—then chaos. All begin to race about discovering their own special interests in the new home, the camera catching but not following WALTER's *discreet disappearance for a few moments.* LENA *goes to the stove and begins to work the oven door with wonder as it pops down and back into place like a dream; there are shouts of exclamatory appreciations now.* TRAVIS *rushes off to the bathroom and is discovered there turning the shower on and off;* BENEATHA *inspects a bedroom;* RUTH *moves into the living room where all the light in the world, it seems to her, cascades in through the uncovered windows.* WALTER *sees her lift her hand once in it and turn it about; he is moved and walks away from her to find enchantment of his own. A shot finds him in the basement inspecting the pipes and heating system with the awkward interest of a man who is unaccustomed to such a setting but who is rapidly feeling at home in it.* RUTH *discovers him there and he looks up to see her. She comes to him and they do not say anything to one another but cling quite close together. Then:*

TWO SHOT—

RUTH AND WALTER EMERGING FROM
BASEMENT, THEIR ARMS ABOUT
ONE ANOTHER

RUTH: Where'd you put them?

WALTER: In the backyard. Let's get her out there. *(Loudly:)* What you say we go out and have a look at the backyard, Old Moms.

MED. CLOSE SHOT—LENA AT SINK,
TESTING SPIGOTS

LENA: I'll "old Moms" you!

FULL SHOT

She turns from the sink and joins them, as do TRAVIS *and* BENEATHA. *They open the back door and look out at the yard. A panning shot shows it to be small and tidy and grassless, true to the season. An area along the fence walls is turned-earth, signifying that flowers are to grow there.* LENA *looks out and her eyes come to rest on:*

STATIONARY SHOT—GIFT-WRAPPED BOX *sitting in the yard. It is the large box with a big shiny red ribbon around it that* RUTH *had busied herself so ostentatiously guarding and getting on the premises as the others ushered* LENA *ahead. On it sits the second, smaller one entrusted to* BENEATHA *and eagerly watched by* TRAVIS. *Although* LENA *knows that both are for her, she has no way of knowing the character of the gifts.*

GROUP SHOT—IN DOORWAY

All watch LENA *to enjoy the surprise they have prepared for her.*

> LENA: What is that?

> WALTER *(enjoying himself)*: Oh, just a little something! *(Then, sweetly:)* Go 'head, Mama, open it. It's for you. . . .

LENA *looks at all of them with loving suspicion and then starts out to the offerings.*

MED. CLOSE—LENA *picking up smaller box. She opens it and lifts out, one by one, a complete set of brand-new gardening tools. Her children move into the scene around her.*

> WALTER: Read the note—Ruth made it up.

LENA *fishes into the wrappings and comes up with the note as* BENEATHA *helps her to find her glasses and get them on. She holds the note out and reads innocently:*

> LENA: "To our own Mrs. Miniver—Love from Brother, Ruth, and Beneatha." Ain't that lovely?

TRAVIS *immediately begins to tug at his father's sleeve.*

> TRAVIS: Can I give her mine now, Daddy?

> WALTER: All right, Son.

TRAVIS *awkwardly lifts* his *gift to give to his grandmother himself.*

> Travis didn't go in with the rest of us, Mama. He got his own—we don't even know what it is.

GROUP SHOT

> LENA *(anticipating)*: Lord, baby, you done bought your grandmother a hat?

> TRAVIS *(beside himself with eagerness)*: Open it!

LENA *does so and lifts out an elaborate—very elaborate— wide gardening hat. All the adults except* LENA *fold over with laughter at the sight of it.*

> RUTH: Travis, honey, what is that?

> TRAVIS *(in earnest)*: It's a gardening hat! The kind the ladies always have on in the magazines when they work in their gardens.

> BENEATHA *(giggling fiercely)*: Travis, we were trying to make Mama Mrs. Miniver—not Scarlett O'Hara!

LENA *(indignantly, in her grandson's behalf)*: What's the matter with you all? This here is a beautiful hat! *(Absurdly:)* Always wanted me one just like it!

She then pops it on her head to prove the point. It is oversized and ludicrous.

RUTH: Hot dog—go, Lena!

WALTER: I'm sorry, Mama *(he is doubled over at the sight)*, but you look like you ready to go out and chop you some cotton, sure enough!

They laugh uproariously, except for LENA. *Still out of deference to her grandson's feelings, she gathers him into her arms and chides the others.*

LENA: Don't you pay 'em a bit of mind, baby. This here is a beautiful hat, that's what!

RUTH, WALTER, *and* BENEATHA *chime in, noisily and festively to insincerely congratulate the boy on his perfectly ridiculous gift.*

LENA: You help me take these things down in the basement. Next spring I'm going to show you how we used to grow 'zaleas down home. . . .

The two of them start to bustle with the equipment. WALTER, RUTH, *and* BENEATHA *continue the tease and the laughter. At the apex of mellowness,* WALTER *reaches out and slips one arm about his wife and holds her close.* RUTH *looks up at him in her own happiness.* WALTER *sighs a bit and looks about at the backyards of his new neighborhood.*

CLOSE SHOT—WALTER'S FACE *still caught with satisfaction—which is suddenly arrested. Slowly his lips close and his eyes narrow as he turns his head slowly, surveying the windows of the houses around them. Then the lips tighten, as do, we feel, the tissues of his body.*

MED. CLOSE SHOT—RUTH, WALTER

RUTH, *who is looking up at him, notices the change and looks out to see what he sees.*

PANNING SHOT—P.O.V.: WALTER AND RUTH

The camera roams at medium close over the surrounding houses. There is an imposed starkness in the shot, reflecting these surroundings as they seem to Ruth and Walter. These are American homes where rather ordinary types and varieties of Americans live; but at the moment something sinister clings to them. At some windows curtains drop back quickly into place, as though those who are watching do not want to be seen; at others, shadowy figures simply move back out of view when they feel that Walter and Ruth's gaze is upon them; at still others, those who are staring do so without apology. The faces—the eyes of women and children, in the main—look hard with a curiosity that, for the most part, is clearly hostile.

MED. CLOSE SHOT—RUTH, WALTER *as before.* WALTER *looks down at his wife and they exchange a look of total understanding. The woman shrugs a little helplessly. There is nothing to say. He smiles at her and they turn and walk back to the house,* TRAVELING SHOT:

Shot goes with them. The voices of LENA and TRAVIS offscreen from the basement identify their preoccupation with arranging the gardening tools and other chatter that indicates they are unaware of the qualitative change of mood that momentarily affected WALTER and RUTH.

QUICK FLASH—MED. CLOSE—BENEATHA STILL IN YARD *where she has noticed what her brother and sis-*

ter-in-law were looking at. She feels a twentieth-century urge to ridicule absurdity and suddenly lifts one hand and stands alone, turning about, waving at the silent watchers, shouting merrily:

BENEATHA: Howdy do! Howdy do!

FADE OUT

FADE IN:

EXTREME CLOSE-UP OF BENEATHA'S HAND NAILING CRATE

Camera moves back to wider angle to include part of living room.

INT.—YOUNGER LIVING ROOM—DAY— FULL SCENE—BENEATHA, RUTH

They are absolutely surrounded by crates, cartons, and stacked furniture.

RUTH: Where are the pots?

BENEATHA: In here.

RUTH *(exasperated)*: And you've nailed it up?

BENEATHA: Didn't you tell me to nail it? I expressly heard you say nail it up.

RUTH: But I did not tell you to put the pots in there with your mother's good china. Common sense ought to tell anybody over seven years old not to pack no heavy pots in with no dishes!

GENERAL SCENE—LONG SHOT

WALTER *enters. His happiness is deep in him; he cannot keep still with his newfound exuberance. He is singing and wiggling and snapping his fingers. He puts a phonograph record, which he has brought with him, on the record player. As the music comes up, he dances over to* RUTH *and tries to get her to dance with him. She gives in to him at last and in a fit of giggling allows herself to be drawn into his mood, and together they deliberately burlesque an old social dance of their youth.*

MED. CLOSE SHOT—BENEATHA WATCHING THEM

> BENEATHA: Talk about ollllld-faaaaaashioned Negroes!

MED. CLOSE—WALTER, RUTH

> WALTER *(stopping momentarily)*: What kind of Negroes?

GENERAL SCENE—GROUP

> BENEATHA: Old-fashioned. *(She imitates them.)*

> WALTER *(as he dances with* RUTH*)*: You know, when these *New Negroes* have their convention *(pointing at his sister)*, that is going to be the chairman of the Committee on Unending Agitation. *(He goes on dancing, then stops.)* Race, race, race! . . . Girl, I do believe you are the first person in the history of the entire human race to successfully brainwash yourself.

BENEATHA *breaks up and he goes on dancing. He stops again, enjoying his tease.*

WALTER: Damn, even the N double-A C P takes a holiday sometimes!

BENEATHA *and* RUTH *laugh. He dances with* RUTH *some more and starts to laugh and stops and pantomimes someone over an operating table.*

WALTER: I can just see that chick someday looking down at some poor cat on an operating table before she starts to slice him, saying *(pulling his sleeves back maliciously)*, "By the way, what are your views on civil rights down there?"

He laughs at her again and starts to dance happily. The bell sounds.

BENEATHA *(moving toward door)*: Sticks and stones may break my bones but . . . words will never hurt me!

MED. CLOSE SHOT—DOOR

BENEATHA *is somewhat surprised to see a quiet-looking middle-aged white* MAN *in a business suit, holding his hat and a briefcase in his hand and consulting a small piece of paper.* KARL LINDNER *might have been an inquiring insurance salesman seeking to gain new clients or for that matter an unobtrusive man of the cloth.*

LINDNER: Uh—how do you do, miss. I am looking for a Mrs.— *(He looks at the slip of paper.)* Mrs. Lena Younger?

WIDER ANGLE TO INCLUDE WALTER, RUTH, STILL CLOWNING

BENEATHA *(smoothing her hair with slight embarrassment)*: Oh—yes, that's my mother. Excuse me. *(She closes the door and turns to quiet the other two.)* Ruth! Brother! Somebody's here.

The music stops. She opens the door. The man casts a curious quick glance at all of them.

Uh—come in, please.

LINDNER *(coming in)*: Thank you.

BENEATHA: My mother isn't here just now. Is it business?

QUICK FLASH—CLOSE—LINDNER

LINDNER: Yes . . . well, of a sort.

GENERAL SCENE—WALTER, RUTH,
BENEATHA, LINDNER

WALTER *(freely, the man of the house)*: Have a seat. I'm Mrs. Younger's son. I look after most of her business matters.

RUTH *and* BENEATHA *exchange amused glances.*

LINDNER *(regarding* WALTER *and sitting)*: Well—my name is Karl Lindner.

WALTER *(stretching out his hand)*: Walter Younger. This is my wife—

RUTH *nods politely.*

—and my sister.

LINDNER: How do you do.

WALTER *(amiably, as he sits himself easily on a chair, leaning forward and looking expectantly into the newcomer's face)*: What can we do for you, Mr. Lindner?

LINDNER *(some minor shuffling of the hat and briefcase on his knees)*: Well—I am a representative of the Clybourne Park Improvement Association—

WALTER *(pointing)*: Why don't you sit your things on the floor?

LINDNER: Oh—yes. Thank you. *(He slides the briefcase and hat under the chair.)* And as I was saying—I am from the Clybourne Park Improvement Association, and we have had it brought to our attention at the last meeting that you people—or at least your mother—has bought a piece of residential property at—*(He digs for a slip of paper.)* —406 Clybourne Street . . .

WALTER: That's right. Care for something to drink? Ruth, get Mr. Lindner a beer.

LINDNER *(upset for some reason)*: Oh—no, really. I mean, thank you very much, but no thank you.

RUTH *(innocently)*: Some coffee?

LINDNER: Thank you, nothing at all.

BENEATHA *is watching the man carefully.*

Well, I don't know how much you folks know about our organization. *(He is a gentleman;*

*thoughtful and somewhat labored in his man-
ner.)* It is one of these community organizations
set up to look after—oh, you know, things like
block upkeep and special projects—and we also
have what we call our New Neighbors Orienta-
tion Committee. . . .

CLOSE SHOT—BENEATHA

BENEATHA *(dryly)*: Yes—and what do they do?

MED. CLOSE—LINDNER

LINDNER *(turning a little to her and then returning
the main force to* WALTER*)*: Well—it's what you
might call a sort of welcoming committee, I
guess. I mean they—we—I'm the chairman of the
committee—go around and see the new people
who move into the neighborhood and sort of give
them the lowdown on the way we do things out
in Clybourne Park.

CLOSE SHOT—BENEATHA

BENEATHA *(with appreciation of the two mean-
ings, which escape* RUTH *and* WALTER*)*: Un-huh.

CLOSE SHOT—LINDNER

LINDNER: And we also have the category of what
the association calls—*(he looks elsewhere)*—uh—
special community problems. . . .

GENERAL SCENE, TO INCLUDE RUTH,
WALTER

BENEATHA: Yes—and what are some of those?

WALTER: Girl, let the man talk.

LINDNER (*with understated relief*): Thank you. I would sort of like to explain this thing in my own way. I mean, I want to explain to you in a certain way.

WALTER: Go ahead.

LINDNER: Yes. Well. I'm going to try to get right to the point. I'm sure we'll all appreciate that in the long run.

BENEATHA: Yes.

WALTER: Be still now!

LINDNER: Well—

RUTH (*still innocently*): Would you like another chair? You don't look comfortable.

LINDNER (*more frustrated than annoyed*): No, thank you very much. Please. Well—to get right to the point, I—(*A great breath and he is off at last.*) I am sure you people must be aware of some of the incidents which have happened in various parts of the city when colored people have moved into certain areas.

BENEATHA *exhales heavily and starts tossing a piece of fruit up and down in the air.*

Well—because we have what I think is going to be a unique type of organization in American community life—not only do we deplore that kind of thing, but we are trying to do something about it.

BENEATHA *stops tossing and turns with a new and quizzical interest to the man.*

We feel—*(gaining confidence in his mission because of the interest in the faces of the people he is talking to)*—we feel that most of the trouble in this world, when you come right down to it—*(he hits his knee for emphasis)*—most of the trouble exists because people just don't sit down and talk to each other.

CLOSE SHOT—LINDNER

JUXTAPOSE CLOSE-UP—RUTH

RUTH *(nodding as she might in church, pleased with the remark)*: You can say that again, mister.

MED. CLOSE—GROUP

LINDNER *(more encouraged by such affirmation)*: That we don't try hard enough in this world to understand the other fellow's problem. The other guy's point of view.

RUTH: Now that's right.

BENEATHA *and* WALTER *merely watch and listen with genuine interest.*

LINDNER: Yes—that's the way we feel out in Clybourne Park. And that's why I was elected to come here this afternoon and talk to you people—friendly-like, you know, the way people should talk to each other—and see if we couldn't find some way to work this thing out. As I say, the whole business is a matter of *caring* for the other fellow. Anybody can see that you are a nice family of folks, hardworking and honest, I'm sure.

BENEATHA *frowns slightly, quizzically, her head tilted, regarding him.*

Today everybody knows what it means to be on the outside of *something*. And of course, there is always somebody who is out to take advantage of people who don't always understand.

WALTER: What do you mean?

LINDNER: Well—you see, our community is made up of people who've worked hard as the dickens for years to build up that little community. They're not rich and fancy people; just hardworking, honest people who don't really have much but those little homes and a dream of the kind of community they want to raise their children in. Now, I don't say we are perfect, and there is a lot wrong in some of the things they want. But you've got to admit that a man, right or wrong in some of the things, has the right to want to have the neighborhood he lives in a certain kind of way. And at the moment the overwhelming majority of our people out there feel that people get along better and take more of a common interest in the life of the community, when they share a common background. I want you to believe me when I tell you that race prejudice simply doesn't enter into it. It is a matter of the people of Clybourne Park believing, rightly or wrongly, as I say, that for the happiness of all concerned that our Negro families are happier when they live in their *own* communities.

EXTREME CLOSE-UP—BENEATHA

BENEATHA *(with a grand and bitter gesture)*: This, friends, is the Welcoming Committee!

GROUP SHOT

WALTER *(dumbfounded, looking at Lindner)*: Is this what you came marching all the way over here to tell us?

LINDNER: Well now, we've been having a fine conversation. I hope you'll hear me all the way through.

WALTER *(tightly)*: Go ahead, man.

LINDNER: You see—in the face of all the things I have said, we are prepared to make your family a very generous offer. . . .

BENEATHA: Thirty pieces and not a coin less!

WALTER: Yeah?

LINDNER *(putting on his glasses and drawing a form out of the briefcase)*: Our association is prepared, through the collective effort of our people, to buy the house from you at a financial gain to your family.

RUTH: Lord have mercy, ain't this the living gall!

WALTER: All right, you through?

LINDNER: Well, I want to give you the exact terms of the financial arrangement.

LOW-ANGLED SHOT—CLOSE—WALTER

WALTER: We don't want to hear no exact terms of no arrangements. I want to know if you got any more to tell us 'bout getting together.

GROUP SHOT

LINDNER (taking off his glasses): Well, I don't suppose that you feel . . .

WALTER: Never mind how I feel—you got any more to say 'bout how people ought to sit down and talk to each other? . . . Get out of my house, man. (He turns his back and walks to the door.)

CLOSE-UP—LINDNER

LINDNER (looking around at the hostile faces and reaching and assembling his hat and briefcase): Well—I don't understand why you people are reacting this way. What do you think you are going to gain by moving into a neighborhood where you just aren't wanted and where some elements—well—people can get awful worked up when they feel that their whole way of life and everything they've ever worked for is threatened.

CLOSE-UP—WALTER

WALTER: Get out.

GENERAL SCENE—GROUP

LINDNER (*at the door, holding a small card*):
Well—I'm sorry it went like this.

WALTER: Get out.

EXTREME CLOSE-UP—LINDNER

LINDNER (*almost sadly regarding Walter*): You
just can't force people to change their hearts,
son.

He turns and puts his card on a table and exits.

GENERAL SCENE

WALTER *pushes the door closed with stinging hatred and
stands looking at it.* RUTH *just sits and* BENEATHA *just
stands. They say nothing.* LENA *and* TRAVIS *enter.*

LENA: Well—this all the packing got done since
I left out of here this morning? I testify before
God that my children got all the energy of the
dead. What time the moving men due?

BENEATHA: Four o'clock. You had a caller,
Mama. (*She is smiling, teasingly.*)

LENA: Sure enough—who?

BENEATHA (*her arms folded saucily*): The Welcoming Committee.

WALTER *and* RUTH *giggle.*

LENA (*innocently*): Who?

BENEATHA: The Welcoming Committee. They said they're sure going to be glad to see you when you get there.

WALTER *(devilishly)*: Yeah, they said they can't hardly wait to see your face.

Laughter.

MED. CLOSE—LENA

LENA *(sensing their facetiousness)*: What's the matter with you all?

WIDER ANGLE TO INCLUDE GROUP

WALTER: Ain't nothing the matter with us. We just telling you 'bout the gentleman who came to see you this afternoon. From the Clybourne Park Improvement Association.

LENA: What he want?

RUTH *(in the same mood as* BENEATHA *and* WALTER*)*: To welcome you, honey.

WALTER: He said they can't hardly wait. He said the one thing they don't have, that they just *dying* to have out there, is a fine family of colored people! *(To* RUTH *and* BENEATHA:*)* Ain't that right!

RUTH and BENEATHA *(mockingly)*: Yeah! He left his card in case—

They indicate the card. LENA *picks it up and throws it on the floor, understanding, and looks off as she draws her*

*chair up to the table on which she has put her plant and
some sticks and some cord.*

EXTREME CLOSE-UP—LENA

> LENA: Father give us strength. *(Knowingly and
> without fun:)* Did he threaten us?

GENERAL SCENE—GROUP

> BENEATHA: Oh—Mama. They don't do it like
> that anymore. He talked Brotherhood. He said
> everybody ought to learn how to sit down and
> hate each other with good Christian fellowship.

She and WALTER *shake hands to ridicule the remark.*

> LENA *(sadly)*: Lord, protect us . . .

> RUTH: You should hear the money those folks
> raised to buy the house from us. All we paid and
> then some.

> BENEATHA: What they think we going to do—
> eat 'em?

CLOSE SHOT—RUTH

> RUTH: No, honey—marry 'em.

MED. CLOSE—GROUP

> LENA *(shaking her head)*: Lord, Lord, Lord . . .

> RUTH: Well—that's the way the crackers crum-
> ble. Joke.

BENEATHA (*laughingly noticing what her mother is doing*): Mama, what are you doing?

LENA: Fixing my plant so it won't get hurt none on the way.

BENEATHA: Mama, you going to take *that* to the new house?

LENA: Un-huh.

BENEATHA: That raggedy-looking old thing?

EXTREME CLOSE-UP—LENA

LENA (*stopping and looking at her*): It expresses *me*.

GENERAL SCENE—GROUP

RUTH (*with delight, to* BENEATHA): So there, Miss Thing!

WALTER *comes to* LENA *suddenly and bends down behind her and squeezes her in his arms with all his strength. She is overwhelmed by the suddenness of it, and, though she is delighted, her manner is like that of* RUTH *with* TRAVIS.

LENA: Look out now, boy! You make me mess up my thing here!

TWO SHOT—LENA, WALTER

WALTER (*his face lit, he slips down on his knees beside her, his arms still about her*): Mama . . . you know what it means to climb up in the chariot?

LENA (*gruffly, very happy*): Get on away from me now. . . .

WALTER: What the old song say, Mama? (*Speaking the lines, sweetly, playfully, in his mother's face:*) I got wings . . . you got wings . . . All God's children got wings . . .

LENA: Boy—get out of my face and do some work. . . .

GENERAL SCENE—GROUP

LENA: What are we all standing around here for? We ain't finished packin' yet. Bennie, you ain't packed one book.

The bell rings.

BENEATHA: That couldn't be the movers . . . it's hardly two yet.

BENEATHA *goes into her room.* LENA *starts for the door.*

EXTREME CLOSE-UP—WALTER

WALTER (*turning, stiffening*): Wait—wait—I'll get it. (*He stands and looks at the door.*)

MED. CLOSE, ANGLED TO INCLUDE RUTH IN BACKGROUND

LENA: You expecting company, Son?

WALTER (*just looking at the door*): Yeah—yeah . . .

LENA *looks at* RUTH, *and they exchange innocent and unfrightened glances.*

LENA (*not understanding*): Well, let them in, Son.

BENEATHA'S VOICE (*offscreen, from her room*): We need some more string.

LENA: Travis—you run to the hardware and get me some string cord.

LENA *goes out.* TRAVIS *goes to a dish for money.* WALTER *turns and looks at* RUTH.

RUTH: Why don't you answer the door, man?

WALTER (*suddenly bounding across the floor to her*): 'Cause sometimes it hard to let the future begin! (*Stooping down in her face:*) I got wings! You got wings! All God's children got wings!

He crosses to the door and throws it open. A wilted BOBO *is standing there rather incongruously dressed in a not-too-prosperous business suit, his eyes haunted and frightened and with a hat pulled down tightly, brim up, around his forehead.* TRAVIS *passes between the two men and exits. In his jubilance,* WALTER *is unaware of* BOBO's *lack of it. Smiling broadly, he leans into the other's face with his song—"When I get to heaven gonna put on my wings/gonna fly all over God's heaven."*

BOBO *just stares at him.*

Heaven—

WALTER *suddenly stops and looks past* BOBO *into the empty hallway.*

Where's Willy, man?

MED. CLOSE—BOBO

> BOBO: He ain't with me.

WIDER ANGLE TO INCLUDE WALTER

> WALTER (*not disturbed*): Oh—come on in. You
> know my wife.

MOVE BACK TO SHOW BOBO ENTERING
APARTMENT

> BOBO (*dumbly, taking off his hat*): Yes—h'you,
> Miss Ruth.

> RUTH (*quietly, a mood apart from her husband
> already, seeing* BOBO): Hello, Bobo.

> WALTER: You right on time today . . . right on
> time. That's the way! (*He slaps* BOBO *on his
> back.*) Sit down . . . lemme hear.

RUTH *stands stiffly and quietly in back of them, as though
somehow she senses death, her eyes fixed on her husband.*

> BOBO (*his frightened eyes on the floor, his hat in
> his hands*): Could I please get a drink a water,
> before I tell you about it, Walter Lee?

WALTER *does not take his eyes off the man.* RUTH *goes
blindly to the tap and gets a glass of water and brings it to*
BOBO.

CLOSE SHOT—WALTER

> WALTER: There ain't nothing wrong, is there?

QUICK FLASH—BOBO

BOBO: Lemme tell you—

CLOSE-UP—WALTER

WALTER: Man—didn't nothing go wrong?

CLOSE-UP—BOBO

BOBO: Lemme tell you—Walter Lee. *(Looking at the floor:)* You know how it was. I got to tell you how it was. I mean, first I got to tell you how it was all the way . . . I mean about the money I put in, Walter Lee. . . .

CLOSE-UP—WALTER

WALTER *(with taut agitation now)*: What about the money you put in?

TWO SHOT—WALTER, BOBO

BOBO: Well—it wasn't much as we told you—me and Willy— *(He stops.)* I'm sorry, Walter. I got a bad feeling about it. I got a real bad feeling about it. . . .

WALTER: Man, what you telling me about all this for? . . . Tell me what happened in Springfield.

BOBO: Springfield.

WIDER ANGLE—TO INCLUDE RUTH

RUTH *(like a dead woman)*: What was supposed to happen in Springfield?

BOBO *(to her)*: This deal that me and Walter went into with Willy—me and Willy was going to go down to Springfield and spread some money round so's we wouldn't have to wait so long for the liquor license. . . . That's what we were going to do. Everybody said that was the way you had to do, you understand, Miss Ruth?

WALTER: Man—what happened down there?

BOBO *(A pitiful man, near tears)*: I'm trying to tell you, Walter.

WALTER *(screaming at him suddenly)*: THEN TELL ME, GOD DAMN IT . . . WHAT'S THE MATTER WITH YOU?

BOBO: Man . . . I didn't go to no Springfield yesterday.

WALTER *(halted, life hanging in the moment)*: Why not?

BOBO *(the long way, the hard way to tell)*: 'Cause I didn't have no reasons to. . . .

WALTER: Man, what are you talking about!

BOBO: I'm talking about the fact that when I got to the train station yesterday morning—eight o'clock like we planned . . . man—*Willy didn't never show up.*

WALTER: Why? . . . Where was he? . . . Where is he?

BOBO: That's what I'm trying to tell you . . . I don't know . . . I waited six hours. . . . I called his house . . . and I waited . . . six hours . . . I waited in that train station six hours. . . . *(Breaking into tears:)* That was all the extra money I had in the world. . . . *(Looking up at* WALTER *with the tears running down his face:)* Man, *Willy is gone.*

EXTREME CLOSE-UP—WALTER

WALTER: Gone? What you mean Willy is gone? Gone where? You mean he went by himself. You mean he went off to Springfield by himself—to take care of getting the license—you mean maybe he didn't want too many people in on the business down there? You know Willy got his own ways. Maybe you was late yesterday and he just went on down there without you. Maybe— maybe—he's been callin' you at home tryin' to tell you what happened or something. Maybe— maybe—he just got sick. He's somewhere—he's got to be somewhere. We just got to find him— me and you got to find him. We got to!

FULL SHOT—WALTER, BOBO, RUTH

BOBO *(in sudden angry, frightened agony)*: What's the matter with you, Walter! *When a cat take off with your money he don't leave you no maps!*

LONG SHOT—HIGH ANGLE—PAST RUTH IN FOREGROUND

WALTER *(turning madly, as though he is looking for Willy in that very room)*: Willy! . . . Willy . . . don't do it. . . . Please don't do it. . . Man, not with that money . . . Man, please, not with that money. . . . Oh, God . . . don't let it be true. . . .

(*He is wandering around crying out for Willy and looking for him or perhaps for help from God.*) Man . . . I trusted you. . . . Man, I put my life in your hands. . . .

He starts to crumple down on the floor as RUTH *just covers her face in horror.* LENA *opens the door and comes into the room with* BENEATHA *behind her.*

Man . . . (*He starts to pound the floor with his fists, sobbing wildly.*) That money is made out of my father's flesh. . . .

BOBO (*standing over him helplessly*): I'm sorry, Walter. . . .

Only WALTER'S *sobs reply.* BOBO *puts on his hat.*

I had my life staked on this deal, too. . . .

He exits.

MED. CLOSE—LENA

LENA (*to* WALTER): Son . . . (*She goes to him, bends down to him, talks to his bent head.*) Son . . . is it gone? Son, I gave you sixty-five hundred dollars. Is it gone? All of it? Beneatha's money too?

FULL SHOT—GROUP

WALTER (*lifting his head slowly*): Mama . . . I never . . . went to the bank at all. . . .

LENA (*not wanting to believe him*): You mean . . . your sister's school money . . . you used that too . . . Walter?

WALTER: Yessss! . . . All of it . . . it's all gone. . . .

There is total silence. RUTH *stands with her face covered with her hands;* BENEATHA *leans forlornly against a wall, fingering a piece of red ribbon from* LENA's *gift.* LENA *stops and looks at her son without recognition and then, quite without thinking about it, starts to beat him senselessly in the face.* BENEATHA *goes to them and stops it.*

BENEATHA: Mama!

LENA *stops and looks at both of her children and rises slowly and wanders vaguely, aimlessly away from them.*

MED. CLOSE—GROUP

LENA: I seen . . . him . . . night after night . . . come in . . . and look at that rug . . . and then look at me . . . the red showing in his eyes . . . the veins moving in his head. . . . I seen him grow thin and old before he was forty . . . working and working and working like somebody's old horse . . . killing himself . . . and you—you give it all away in a day. . . .

BENEATHA: Mama—

LENA: Oh, God . . . *(She looks up at Him.)* Look down here—and show me the strength.

BENEATHA: Mama—

LENA *(folding over)*: Strength . . .

BENEATHA *(plaintively)*: Mama . . .

LENA: Strength!

FADE OUT

FADE IN:

INT.—THE YOUNGER LIVING ROOM—MED.
CLOSE—AN HOUR LATER—DAY

RUTH and BENEATHA sit alone in the living room, which
still is cluttered with the now almost ominous packing
crates. Light sifts in which suggests the darkening late
afternoon.

> RUTH: Why don't you take some nice hot coffee
> in to your mother, Bennie?
>
> BENEATHA: I just don't feel like it, Ruth. You
> do it.

RUTH *stares at her sister-in-law helplessly, sighs, then slowly
rises and pours out a cup of coffee and takes it in to her
mother-in-law.*

CLOSE SHOT—BENEATHA

sitting in profound dejection.

PANNING SHOT—THE PACKING CRATES—
P.O.V.: BENEATHA

STATIONARY SHOT—THE DOOR OF WALTER
LEE'S BEDROOM

BENEATHA'S *eyes come to rest on the door behind which
she knows is her brother.*

INT.—MED. CLOSE—WALTER WITHIN THE ROOM *where he is lying on his back staring at the ceiling, having his own ordeal alone.*

CUT TO:

MED. CLOSE SHOT OF BENEATHA IN LIVING ROOM *still staring at his door. The bell sounds. She rises to answer.*

LONG SHOT—HIGH ANGLES TO SHOW TOTAL ASPECT OF LIVING ROOM

as BENEATHA *opens the door and* ASAGAI *enters in vibrant spirits, his arms lifted.*

> ASAGAI: I had some free time so I came over. I thought I might help with the packing. *(Looking and walking about:)* Ah, how I love the look of packing crates! The sight of a household in preparation for a journey! I know that it depresses some people. But for me it is always another feeling. Something so like the flow of life. Do you understand? Movement, progress. It makes me think of Africa.

CLOSE SHOT—BENEATHA

> BENEATHA *(dismally)*: *Africa.*

TWO SHOT

He comes close to her and lifts her chin in his fingers.

> ASAGAI: Well now, what kind of mood is this? I expected to find you full of sunlight today.

(Pause.) Have I told you how much you move me?

She says nothing and looks away.

Is something wrong?

BENEATHA: He gave away the money, Asagai.

ASAGAI: Who gave away what money?

BENEATHA: The insurance money. My brother gave it away.

ASAGAI *(with incredulity)*: Gave it away?

BENEATHA: He would say that he made an *investment*. The only thing is that he made it with a man even Travis wouldn't have trusted with his most worn marbles.

CUT TO:

INT.—WALTER IN BEDROOM, LISTENING

ASAGAI *(offscreen)*: And it is gone?

BENEATHA *(offscreen)*: Gone.

CUT TO:

LIVING ROOM—TWO SHOT—BENEATHA, ASAGAI

ASAGAI: I'm very sorry.

BENEATHA: But Brother is not the crazy one. By his lights he did what made sense to him. No,

Mama is the crazy one. She is the one who got up one fine day and threw away our lives.

ASAGAI: Oh, your mother isn't crazy.

BENEATHA: Oh no? Well, you've met my brother. Would you ever have put that much money in his hands. Ever?

ASAGAI (*smiling*): Perhaps I don't understand some things as well as your mother.

BENEATHA: Oh, God!

ASAGAI: What about you now?

BENEATHA (*catching at her head with her hands*): Me? . . . Me? . . . You know, when you come right down to it it's probably just as well. Why should anyone want to be a doctor in this nutty world!

CLOSE SHOT—BENEATHA

You know, when I was very small we used to take our sleds out in the wintertime, and the only hills we had were the ice-covered stone steps of some houses down the street. And we used to fill them in with snow and make them smooth and slide down them all day. . . . It was very danger-ous, you know, far too steep. . . . And sure enough, one day a kid named Rufus came down too fast and hit the sidewalk . . . and we saw his face just split open right there in front of us. I remember standing there looking at his bloody open face thinking that was the end of Rufus. But the ambulance came and they took him to the hospital and they fixed the broken bones and they sewed it all up . . . and the next time I saw Rufus he just had a little line down the middle of his face. . . . I never got over that. . . .

ASAGAI: What?

CUT TO:

INT.—BEDROOM—CLOSE SHOT—WALTER
sitting up on the bed, head in hands, listening.

BENEATHA *(offscreen)*: That that was what one person could do for another: fix him up—sew up the problem, make him all right again. That was the most marvelous thing in the world—I wanted to do that. I always thought it was the most marvelous thing in the world that a human being could do. Fix up the sick, you know—and make them whole again. This was truly being God. . . .

ASAGAI *(offscreen)*: You wanted to be God?

CUT TO:

LIVING ROOM—TWO SHOT—BENEATHA, ASAGAI

BENEATHA: No—I wanted to *cure*. It used to be so important to me. I mean, about people and how their bodies hurt . . .

ASAGAI: And you've stopped caring?

BENEATHA: Yes—I think so.

ASAGAI: Why?

BENEATHA: Because it doesn't seem deep enough, close enough to what ails mankind—I mean this thing of sewing up bodies and administering drugs. Don't you understand? It was a child's reaction to the world.

ASAGAI: Children see things very well sometimes.

BENEATHA: I know that's what you think. Because you are still where I left off. You with the dreams of the future think you will patch up all Africa. You are going to cure the great sore of colonialism with independence!

ASAGAI: Yes!

BENEATHA: Yes—*and then what?* What about all the crooks and petty thieves and just plain idiots who will come into power to steal and plunder the same as before, only they will be black and do it in the name of the new independence? *What about them?*

ASAGAI: That will be the problem of another time. First we must get there.

BENEATHA: And where does it end?

ASAGAI: End? Who ever spoke of an end? To life? To living?

CLOSE SHOT—BENEATHA

BENEATHA: *An end to misery!* . . . Don't you see there isn't any real progress, Asagai? There is only one large circle that we march in, around and around, each of us with our own little picture in front of us—our own little mirage that we think is the *future*!

ASAGAI: That is the mistake.

BENEATHA: What?

ASAGAI: What you just said—about the circle.

CLOSE SHOT—ASAGAI

It isn't a circle. It is simply a long line—as in geometry, you know, one that reaches into infinity. And because we cannot see the end—we also cannot see how it changes. And it is very odd that those who see the changes are called "idealists," and those who cannot, or refuse to, think they are the "realists"—it is very strange, and amusing too, I think. But you—I never thought to see you in these ranks. Already—and after just one small defeat—you would worship despair?

TWO SHOT

BENEATHA: *Small defeat!* . . . Asagai, this family has been wiped out! What is the matter with you? Don't they use money, for heaven's sake, where you come from?

ASAGAI *reaches out and takes her by the shoulders and turns her full face to him.*

ASAGAI: Look here, my dear, was it your money?

BENEATHA *frowns to understand.*

I said, was it your money that was lost?

CUT TO:

WALTER IN BEDROOM—EXTREME CLOSE-UP

His head is pressed in anguish against the door as he listens.

BENEATHA *(offscreen)*: It belonged to all of us.

ASAGAI *(offscreen)*: Yes, but did you earn it? Would there have been ten thousand dollars in this family if your father had not died?

CUT TO:

LIVING ROOM—TWO SHOT—ASAGAI, BENEATHA

ASAGAI *(still holding her)*: Then isn't this rather all a false funeral?

She just stares at him.

Can't it help you to see that there is something wrong when all the dreams in this house—good or bad—had to depend on something that might never have happened if a man had not died? We always say at home: Accident was at the first and will be at the last a poor tree from which the fruits of life may bloom.

BENEATHA: Oh, is that what you say at home! Ta ta! Well, I've got news! You go home and tell the proverb slingers not to count on that little old idea, because life is only one thing—*silly*.

ASAGAI: I see. Now you are ready to write off the whole human race as a waste. I never thought to see you in such ranks. For all of your keen mind you do not understand the greatness of the thing your mother tried to do. You think she is of the old order because she does things out of blind faith. It does not occur to you that she understands more deeply than you, for all of her ignorance, for all of her groping—that she moves, she acts, she changes things. She is the substance of the human race. You—in your present state—you are but another burden for her. Something to carry along, to bolster. . . .

BENEATHA: I?

ASAGAI: You! Your brother made a stupid, childish mistake—and you are grateful to him. So that now you can give up the whole ailing human race on account of it. All your talk about what good is struggle—what good is anything—where are we all going—and why are we bothering!

BENEATHA: *And you cannot answer it!*

CLOSE SHOT—ASAGAI

ASAGAI: *I live the answer!*

MED. CLOSE SHOT—BENEATHA, ASAGAI

She looks at him with deepening understanding.

ASAGAI: In my village at home it is still the exceptional man who can even read a book. And much worse things still prevail. But those of us who go home will work and teach, and things will happen. Things *will* happen; the sudden dramatic events which make history leap into the future.

Because we make it so. And in all that tumult which is bound to come, even I will have moments when I cannot help but feel that the quiet was better. But then I will look about my village once again at the ignorance and disease and poverty and I will not wonder long. Now, this is what I am trying to tell you, Alaiyo—

CLOSE SHOT—LOW-ANGLED—ASAGAI

Perhaps I may grow to be a great man. I mean, perhaps I shall manage to hold on to the substance of truth and find my way always with the right course. But for which reason I might be butchered in my bed some night by the servants of empire. Or perhaps I shall turn into the kind of leader who will cling to outmoded ways and do terrible things in order to keep my power. Don't you see, there will be young men and women then to step out of the shadow some evening and slit my then useless throat? Not foreign soldiers but my own black countrymen. Don't you see that they have always been there and that they always will be? It is the nature of progress that when I am corrupted—even my own death can be an advance. They who might kill me would actually replenish all that I am right now.

TWO SHOT—BENEATHA, ASAGAI

BENEATHA: Oh, Asagai, I know all of that!

ASAGAI: Good. Then stop moaning and groaning and tell me what you plan to do.

BENEATHA: Do?

ASAGAI: I have a bit of a suggestion.

BENEATHA: What?

ASAGAI: That when it is all over—that you come home with me.

BENEATHA: Oh, Asagai—at a time like this you decide to be romantic!

ASAGAI: My dear young creature of the New World—I do not mean across the city. I mean across the occan—*home*—to Africa.

BENEATHA: To—Nigeria?

ASAGAI: Yes. Three hundred years later the African prince rose up out of the seas and swept the maiden back across the middle passage over which her ancestors had come. . . .

BENEATHA: Nigeria?

ASAGAI: Nigeria. Home. I will show you our mountains and our stars and give you cool drinks from gourds and teach you the old songs and the ways of our people. And, in time, we will pretend that you have only been away for a day.

He takes her in his arms. She allows it a second and then pulls away, confused.

BENEATHA: You're getting me all mixed up. . . .

ASAGAI: Why?

BENEATHA: Too many things. Because just too many things have happened around here today.

I don't know what I feel about anything at this moment. I am going to just sit down and think.

ASAGAI: All right. I shall leave you. No, don't get up. *(He comes over and touches her hair.)* Just sit awhile and think. Never be afraid to just sit awhile and think. *(He goes to door and looks back at her.)* How often I have looked at you and said, "Ah, so this is what the New World hath finally wrought!"

He goes out. BENEATHA *sits on alone. Presently* WALTER *enters from bedroom and starts to rummage through things, feverishly looking for something. She looks up and turns in her seat.*

CLOSE SHOT—BENEATHA

BENEATHA *(hissingly; almost involuntary passion)*: Well, there he is—*Monsieur le petit bourgeois noir* himself! There he is—titan of the system! Did you dream of yachts on Lake Michigan, Brother? Did you see yourself on that great day sitting down at the conference table, surrounded by all the great and mighty bald-headed men in America?

GENERAL SCENE

WALTER *ignores her completely and continues frantically and destructively looking for something and hurling things to floor and tearing things out of their place in his search.* BENEATHA *ignores the eccentricity of his actions and goes on with the monologue of insult.*

All halted, waiting, breathless, waiting for your pronouncements on industry? Waiting for you—chairman of the board?

WALTER *finds what he is looking for—a small piece of white paper—and pushes it into his pocket. He puts on his coat and rushes out without ever having looked at her. Beneatha shouts after him.*

I look at you and I see the final triumph of stupidity in the world!

The door slams.

CLOSE SHOT—RUTH *near the sofa where* TRAVIS *sleeps.*

RUTH: Who was that?

GENERAL SCENE—RUTH, BENEATHA

BENEATHA: Your husband.

RUTH: Where did he go?

BENEATIIA: Who knows—maybe he had an appointment at U.S. Steel.

RUTH *(anxiously, with frightened eyes)*: You didn't say nothing bad to him, did you?

BENEATHA: Bad? Say anything bad to him? No—I told him he was a sweet boy and full of dreams and everything is strictly peachy keen.

The bedroom door opens at the other side and LENA comes out. She has obviously made the supreme effort to compose herself, artificially. She smiles lamely, unconvincingly at the two women and goes to her plant, which is still sitting where she left it in happier moments. She looks at it and picks it up and takes it to the window and puts it back on the sill.

Then she closes the window, straightens her body with a sigh, and turns around to face her children.

> LENA: Well now—ain't it a mess in here! I guess we better all stop moping around and get some work done. Where's Brother? He can start opening up these crates. One of you all better call the moving men and tell 'em not to come.

> RUTH: Tell 'em not to come?

> LENA: Of course, baby—ain't no need of 'em coming all the way here and then having to go back. They charges for that too. *(She sits, fingers to her brow, thinking.)*

CLOSE SHOT—LENA

> Lord, ever since I was a little girl, I always remembers people saying, "Lena—Lena Eggleston, you aims too high all the time. You needs to slow down and see life a little more like it is. Just slow down some." That's what they always used to say down home—"Lord, that Lena Eggleston is a high-minded thing. She'll get her due one day!"

> RUTH: No, Lena . . .

> LENA: Me and Big Walter just didn't never learn right.

MED. CLOSE—RUTH, BENEATHA, LENA *who has sat down on the couch and given up the entire family.* RUTH *turns to her.*

> RUTH *(hysterically)*: No! Bennie—tell her, you tell her! We can still move—the notes ain't but a

hundred and twenty-five a month. . . . We got four grown people in this house . . . we can work . . . we can all work! Lena—I'll work . . . I'll work twenty hours a day, in all the kitchens in Chicago. I'll strap my baby on my back if I have to, and scrub all the floors in America and wash all the sheets in America if I have to! But we got to move . . . we got to get out of here.

LENA: No—I sees things differently now. This ain't the time for us to be trying to take on nothing like that. I'm already thinking 'bout some of the things we could do to fix this here place up some. . . . I seen a secondhand bureau over on Maxwell Street the other day that could fit right there! Just need some new handles and a little varnish and it look brand-new. And, why, Walter could get some screens and put them up in your room around the baby's bassinet. *(She looks at both of them, pleadingly.)* Sometimes you just got to know when to give up some things . . . and hold on to what you got.

The camera focuses on WALTER *entering from the outside, looking spent and leaning against the door, his coat hanging from him.*

MED. CLOSE—LENA, WALTER, BENEATHA, RUTH

LENA: Where you been, Son?

WALTER *(Breathing hard)*: Made a call.

LENA: To who, Son?

WALTER: To The Man.

LENA: What man, baby?

WALTER: *The* man, Mama. Don't you know who The Man is? Bennie—you a hip little girl—tell her who The man is!

BENEATHA *(with sudden realization)*: Lindner!

WALTER: That's right! That's right! That's very good. See there, like I told you—this is a very smart little girl. She knows everything!

BENEATHA: What do you want to see him for?

WALTER: We going to do business with him. I told him to come right on over.

LENA: What you talking about, Son?

WALTER: Talkin 'bout life, Mama. Ain't you always telling me to see life like it is? Well, I'm doing it! I understood it down there on my knees a little while ago—*LIFE*. . . . I saw it in a vision. Just what life is. . . . Finally figured out why some people in this world are always being taken. It's just some people—it ain't everybody. *(He laughs bitterly.)* People like Willy Harris, for instance—they don't never get taken. You know why the rest of us do? Because we are mixed up—I mean we are mixed up, *bad!* We spend our lives out here lookin' for the right and the wrong of everything. The Right and the Wrong. We worry about it and cry about it and stay up nights trying to figure out the right and the wrong of things—and all the time, boy, them takers are out there operatin'—just takin' and takin' and takin'. Like old Willy Harris. But I'll say one thing for old Willy Harris—he sure taught me to put my eye on what counts in this world! Thanks, old buddy—I ain't never gonna forget!

RUTH: What did you call that man for, Walter Lee?

WALTER: Called him to tell him to come on over to the show. We goin' to put on a show for him— just what he wants to see!

RUTH: You talkin' about taking them people's money to keep us from moving into that house!

WALTER: Another smart girl! I ain't just talkin' about it, baby—I'm telling you that that is what is going to happen.

LENA: You makin' an awful pain inside me, son. You makin' something inside me cry.

WALTER: Don't cry, Mama—understand. That white man is going to walk in that door able to write checks for more money than we ever had. It's important to him. And I'm going to help him—I'm going to put on the show!

CLOSE SHOT—LOW-ANGLED—LENA'S FACE

LENA: Walter Lee—I come from five generations of slaves and sharecroppers—and ain't nobody in my family never let nobody pay 'em no money that was a way of telling us we wasn't fit to walk the earth. We ain't never been that poor—and we ain't never been that dead inside.

CLOSE SHOT—WALTER

WALTER: What's the matter with you all? I didn't make this world! It was give to me this way! Hell yes *(to his sister)*, I want me some yachts someday! Yes, I want to hang some real pearls round my wife's neck! Ain't she supposed to wear no pearls? Somebody tell me *who* it is who decides which women is supposed to wear pearls in this world? I tell you, I am a *man*—and I think my wife should wear some pearls in this world!

FULL SCENE

The last line hangs and WALTER *begins to move about the room with enormous agitation, as if the word "man" has set off its own reaction in his mind. He mumbles it to himself as he moves about. The interplay of his conflict is at work now in him, no matter what he says. It is the realization that begins now that will decide his actions to come; thus he is quarreling with* WALTER LEE; *all actions he performs are to persuade himself.*

LENA: Baby, how you going to feel on the inside?

WALTER *(a little madly)*: Fine! . . . Going to feel fine! A man. . . .

LENA *(shaking her head)*: You won't have nothing left in you then, Walter Lee. There is some things that people can do that take the insides out of them. . . .

WALTER: I'm going to feel fine! I'm going to look that man in the eyes and say—*(He falters visibly for the first time.)* I'll say: "All right, Mr. Lindner—" *(He falters again; the persuasion is not easy.)* "That's your neighborhood out there and you got a right to keep it the way you want!" *(He glares at all of them.)* That's right! I'm going to say more than that! Gonna say, "You just write me that check and the house is yours! Yeah, you just put that money in my hand and you won't have to live next door to no bunch of *stinking niggers!*"

His wife and his sister turn away from him, unable to watch. His mother alone keeps her eyes trained on him, watching.

I'll do more than that—I know what the white man loves—I'll *(with final and terrible abandon he acts it out)* get down on my black knees and I'll do the whole show: "Captain, Mistuh, Boss-man! Hee, hee, hee! Great White Father, y'all jes' gi' ussen de money, fo' Gawd's sake, and we's ain't gwine cum out deh and dirty up yo's white folks' neighborhood!"

At the end of the recitation WALTER *breaks down completely. He gets up and goes into the bedroom and quietly closes the door.*

BENEATHA: Well—let's go get the coffin. That is the end of Walter Lee Younger.

LENA: You mourning your brother?

BENEATHA: That is no brother of mine.

LENA: What you say?

BENEATHA: I said that that—individual—in that room is no brother of mine!

LENA (*with a strange quietness; picking out the essentials of the experience over the obvious troubles before them*): Oh? You feeling better than him today? You done give him up for me? Well, who give you that privilege?

BENEATHA: Can't you be on my side for once! You saw what he just did, Mama! You saw him just as plain as me down there on his knees! Well, wasn't it you who taught me to despise any man who would do that—who would do what he's going to do?

LENA: Yes, I taught you that—me and your daddy. But I thought I taught you something else. I thought we taught you to love him. . . .

BENEATHA: There's nothing left to love.

RUTH (*quietly—from across the room—but without a drop of uncertainty in her voice*): There is always something left to love.

LENA (*still to her daughter*): Have you cried for that boy today? I don't mean for yourself and for the family 'cause we lost the money. I mean for him; what he been through and what it done to him. Child, when do you think is the time to love somebody the most—when they done good and made things easy for everybody? Well, then, you ain't through learning—because that ain't the time at all. It's when he's at his lowest and can't believe in hisself 'cause the world done whipped him so. When you starts measuring somebody, measure him right, child, measure him right. Make sure you done taken into account what hills and valleys he come through before he got to wherever he is.

TRAVIS *bursts into the room. He leaves the door open.*

TRAVIS: Grandmama—the moving men are downstairs! The truck just pulled up.

CLOSE SHOT—LENA

LENA *(defeated)*: Are they, baby?

FULL SCENE

LENA *sits down and stares into space, as do* BENEATHA *and* RUTH. TRAVIS *looks from one to another.*

TRAVIS *(to someone)*: Hello.

Each of the adults turns to see whom the child has addressed. Their eyes discover MR. LINDNER, *once again standing in the doorway with briefcase and hat. Each of them turns away, and* RUTH *rises slowly and goes to the door of the bedroom where* WALTER *is.* LINDNER *talks to them as though it were a two-way conversation.*

LINDNER: I came right over.

RUTH *(to* WALTER *in the room)*: He's here.

LINDNER *goes to the table and opens his briefcase and starts to unfold papers and unscrew fountain pens and do other little busy things like that. If a mood in the room penetrates his consciousness he has come predisposed to ignore it.*

LINDNER: Well, I was certainly glad to hear from you people. Life can really be so much easier than people let it be most of the time. *(A small pleasant chuckle follows that assessment of the nature of life. It falls in the quiet.)*

WALTER *appears in the doorway. The tumult of the moments just past that raged through him has disappeared. The roar of determination of his previous spirit has utterly dissolved, and the enormity of his stated intention now faces him with utter simplicity. Nothing remains within him to replace the former bravado of what was to be his imposed degradation. Thus he stands, a little awkwardly in the doorway, not unlike a boy who must superimpose a larger deed on a former small intent. Occasionally he passes his sleeve across his mouth and looks from his wife, who cannot look at him at all, to his sister, who will not look at him—who wishes perhaps that he would be struck dead on the spot— to his mother, who also will not look at him, who sits with her hands folded on her lap and her eyes closed as* WALTER *begins to advance toward the man.* TRAVIS *misses all essences of the moment and wanders to the table to boyishly look at the hateful papers.* LINDNER *is kindly in dismissing him.*

> LINDNER: Just some official papers, sonny. Well, with whom do I negotiate, Mrs. Younger? You or your son here?

RUTH *reaches out suddenly and grabs her boy.*

> RUTH: Travis—you go on downstairs.

LENA *opens her eyes at the remark and without turning gives the order.*

> LENA: No you don't! You stay right here, Travis. And you make him understand what you doin', Walter Lee! You teach him good 'bout what counts in this world—like Willy Harris done taught you. Go on, son, you show your boy what our five generations done come to.

WALTER YOUNGER *looks down into the face of his son, who is standing grinning up at him merrily—seeing signifi-*

cance in none of it. WALTER *looks at him and starts to laugh a little bit and drops his arm lightly, informally about* TRAVIS's *shoulders. Decision is not the problem now—it is only how to tell this stranger who could understand so little as to be there in the first place. And since* WALTER *is a man who is unaccustomed to speaking in affirmatives, it throws him, and embarrasses him—and the strange sensation in his stomach is new to him.*

WALTER: Well . . . Mr. Lindner . . . well, now, we called you here—that is to say, me and my family called you here—on account of *(he shifts from one foot to the other)* we are sort of plain people.

LINDNER: Yes?

WALTER: I mean like what you say you got out in your neighborhood? Well, that's what we are, plain people. *(A deep breath.)* I mean, I work as a chauffeur, and my wife and my mother are domestics—they work in other people's kitchens.

LINDNER *(a little impatiently, a little confused)*: Yes, Mr. Younger, I understand.

WALTER: Well, no, it's not so easy to understand. I mean, my father—geez, my father, he almost beat a man to death once a long time ago on account of this man call him some kind of name or something—you dig?

BENEATHA *turns slowly.*

LINDNER: Yes, that's very interesting—

WALTER: What I mean is *(grinning a little)* I don't know how come, man, but we got all this pride going. You know what I mean? But the fact is—that we called you over here to tell you that—*(seeing* TRAVIS *suddenly and pulling him into it)*—this is my son, and he makes like the sixth generation of my folks in this country, and we have all thought about your offer—yeah—and we—I—have thought about your offer and I have decided that we are going to move into our new house and because—well—my father, he earned it for us, *brick by brick.*

RUTH *is a small woman who stands as tall as the stars at the moment.* BENEATHA *vigorously nods, and* LENA *sits straight on the couch rocking, a little involuntarily, back and forth, her eyes closed as if she is listening to her gospel in church and signifying wordlessly the "amen yes."*

WALTER *(simply, shrugging, feeling a little nuts)*: That's all, dad—we don't want your money.

He turns and walks away from the man with his son. LIND-NER's *jaws are ajar and he looks from one to another as the two younger women grin at him insanely, their eyes glistening. He crosses rapidly to the mother.*

LINDNER: May I appeal to you, Mrs. Younger? You're older and wiser and you know more about the world.

LENA *(rising as one does to dismiss a visitor)*: I am afraid you don't understand. My son said we was going to move, and there ain't nothing left for me to say. *(Shaking her head:)* You know how these young folks is nowadays, mister. Getting so you can't do a thing with 'em. Goodbye.

MR. LINDNER *turns from her and looks about at all of them. Trouble rather larger than that which he thinks he understands rides on his shoulders as he looks at them.*

LINDNER: Well—if you are that final about it—
I guess there is nothing left for me to say. I sure
hope you people know what you are doing.

*He shakes his head and goes out. There is total quiet for a
second, then* RUTH *stirs herself.*

RUTH: Well, if the moving men are here—LET'S
GET THE HELL OUT OF HERE!

LENA: Ain't it the truth! Look at all this here
mess! Ruth, put Travis's good jacket on him. . . .
Walter Lee, fix your tie and tuck in your shirt
. . . you look just like somebody's hoodlum.
Lord have mercy, where is my plant?

*She flies to get it amid the bustlings of the family, who try
hard to ignore the nobility of the past moment. The movers
come in brusquely and start hauling the furniture about with
the indifference of the profession.*

Travis, child, don't go emptyhanded. . . . Ruth,
where did I put that box with my skillets in
it? . . . Beneatha, what's the matter with them
stockins? Pull 'em up, pull 'em up!

The family starts out. BENEATHA *comes away from the
window dreamily, the most immediate events of the past
already forgotten.*

BENEATHA: Mama, you know what I think I'll
do?

LENA *is busy supervising the moving.*

LENA: What, honey?

BENEATHA (*ecstatically, irrelevantly, as she personally gets out her guitar case*): I think—yes—I think I shall marry Asagai and go live in Africa someday!

LENA (*distractedly*): You ain't old enough to marry nobody. (*Noting one of the movers:*) Darlin', that ain't no bale of cotton you got there. I had that chair twenty-five years—please handle it so's we can sit in it again. . . .

The movers sigh with exasperation and go on with their work. WALTER *returns for a second load and overhears his sister.*

BENEATHA: Oh—not now, Mama—but think of all the good I could do! (*Zealousy doth youth speak.*) A doctor—in Africa!

LENA: Yes, honey.

WALTER (*himself—entirely*): Africa! What you want to go to Africa for?

BENEATHA (*happily*): I am thinking I shall someday marry Asagai and go be a doctor in Africa—practice there!

WALTER: Girl, if you don't get all them silly ideas out your head once and for all and start looking round in this world for you a man with some loot, you better! Talkin' bout Africa!

BENENATHA: Oh, what have you got to do with what I do?

WALTER (*missing no opportunity*): I got plenty to do with it. I'm the head of this family and I think you need to marry you somebody like George Murchison. . . .

They go out laughingly, dragging and pushing cartons.

BENEATHA *(screaming at him offscreen)*: George Murchison! I wouldn't marry that narrow-minded little bourgeois if he was Adam and I was Eve!

Their anger is loud and real until it diminishes. RUTH *stands at the door waiting for* LENA, *smiling at her knowingly.* LENA *is fixing her hat at last.*

LENA: Hmmph . . . they're something all right, my children.

RUTH: Yes—they're something. *(Pause.)* Let's go, Lena.

LENA: Yes—I'm coming.

She waves her out. RUTH *understands and begins to leave* LENA *alone.*

Ruth—

RUTH: Yes?

LENA: He come into his manhood today, didn't he? Kind of like the rainbow after the rain.

RUTH *(quietly)*: Yes, Lena.

WALTER *and* BENEATHA *call to them raucously from below.* RUTH *turns and goes out, bidding* LENA *to hurry. Left alone, the woman looks about the walls of what has been her home for many years now, flooding her with mem-*

ories, and a deep heaving emotion arises within her. WAL-TER *appears in the doorway.*

WALTER (*gently*): Mama, why don't you come on.

LENA: I'm coming, I'm coming.

WALTER (*grinning to relieve the moment*): Mama, how we gonna pay for this house?

LENA: Well, I was just thinking the other day that I didn't like not working much as I thought I did. . . . I guess I call Mrs. Holiday in the morning—see if they got somebody else yet. . . .

They suddenly look at each other in a flash of remembrance, and WALTER *turns and goes to the window and gets the plant and comes back and puts it in his mother's hands, and they go out and down the steps—their conversation about the nature of the future going on:* WALTER *suggesting that Charlie Atkins might someday want a partner if he can get the capital together. . . .*

FADE OUT

THE END

PLUME 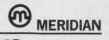 **MERIDIAN**

EXCEPTIONAL PLAYS

(0452)

☐ **FENCES A Play by August Wilson.** The author of the 1984-85 Broadway season's best play, *Ma Rainey's Black Bottom,* return with another powerful, stunning dramatic work. "Always absorbing . . . the work's protagonist—and greatest creation—is a Vesuvius of rage . . . The play's finest moments perfectly capture that inky almost imperceptibly agitated darkness just before the fences of racism, for a time, came crashing down."—Frank Rich, *The New York Times* (264014—$8.00)

☐ **MA RAINEY'S BLACK BOTTOM by August Wilson.** The time is 1927. The place is a run-down recording studio in Chicago where Ma Rainey, the legendary blues singer, is due to arrive. What goes down in the session to come is more than music, it is a riveting portrayal of black rage . . . of racism, of the self-hate that racism breeds, and of racial exploitation. (261139—$7.95)

☐ **A RAISIN IN THE SUN by Lorraine Hansberry.** From one of the most potent voices in the American theater comes A RAISIN IN THE SUN, which touched the taproots of black American life as never before and won the New York Critics Circle Award. This Twenty-Fifth Anniversary edition also includes Hansberry's last play, THE SIGN IN SIDNEY BRUSTEIN'S WINDOW, which became a theater legend. "Changed American theater forever!"—*New York Times* (264855—$10.00)

☐ **BLACK DRAMA ANTHOLOGY Edited by Woodie King and Ron Milner.** Here are twenty-three extraordinary and powerful plays by writers who brought a dazzling new dimension to the American theater. Includes works by Imamu Amiri Baraka (LeRoi Jones), Archie Shepp, Douglas Turner Ward, Langston Hughes, Ed Bullins, Ron Zuber, and many others who gave voice to the anger, passion and pride that shaped a movement, and continue to energize the American theater today. (009022—$7.00)

Prices slightly higher in Canada.

Buy them at your local bookstore or use this convenient coupon for ordering.

NEW AMERICAN LIBRARY
P.O. Box 999, Bergenfield, New Jersey 07621

Please send me the books I have checked above.
I am enclosing $_____ (please add $2.00 to cover postage and handling).
Send check or money order (no cash or C.O.D.'s) or charge by Mastercard or VISA (with a $15.00 minimum).
Prices and numbers are subject to change without notice.

Card # _____ Exp. Date _____
Signature _____
Name _____
Address _____
City _____ State _____ Zip Code _____

For faster service when ordering by credit card call 1-800-253-6476

Allow a minimum of 4-6 weeks for delivery. This offer is subject to change without notice

 Plume

OUTSTANDING DRAMA

0452

☐ **FIVE PLAYS BY MICHAEL WELLER.** With unmatched intimacy and accuracy, this remarkable collection of plays captures the feelings, the dilemmas, the stances, and above all the language of the 1980's. This volume brings together for the first time five of Weller's plays, in their author's final versions.   (261201—$10.95)

☐ **PRELUDE TO A KISS by Craig Lucas.** An award-winning play that transforms a classic romantic fairy tale into a stunningly powerful evocation of sex, death, and compassion in times that are far from compassionate. "Enchanting, charming, mysterious . . . Craig Lucas is a born playwright!" —*The New Yorker*
(265673—$8.00)

☐ **A LIE OF THE MIND by Sam Shepard.** This play fills the stage and mind with a vision that is, in the words of Frank Rich in *The New York Times,* "as wide, long, deep, mysterious and unruly as the Mississippi River—a variously rending and hilarious reverie about parents and sons and husbands and wives, all blending into a mythic wilderness that has served writers from Harte, Twain and Cather to Welty, Didion and McMurty."   (263573—$7.95)

Prices slightly higher in Canada.

Buy them at your local bookstore or use this convenient coupon for ordering.

NEW AMERICAN LIBRARY
P.O. Box 999, Bergenfield, New Jersey 07621

Please send me th
I am enclosing $ d handling).
Send check or m   ) minimum).
Prices and nur

Card # _____
Signature _____
Name _____
Address _____
City _____

Allo   ce